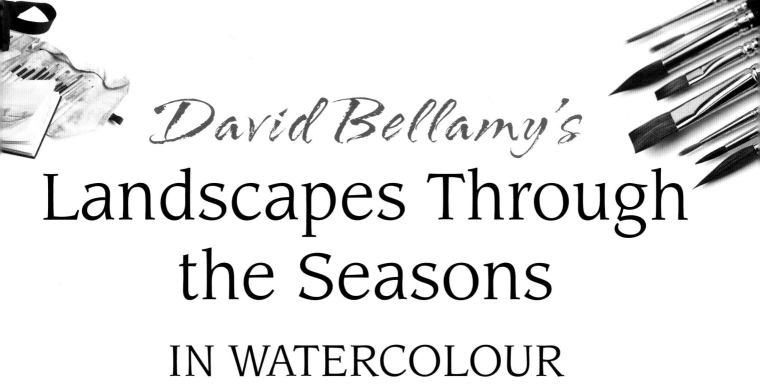

David Bellamy's
Landscapes Through the Seasons
IN WATERCOLOUR

Dedication
To Gwinny, who brings so much sunshine into my life.

David Bellamy's
Landscapes Through the Seasons

IN WATERCOLOUR

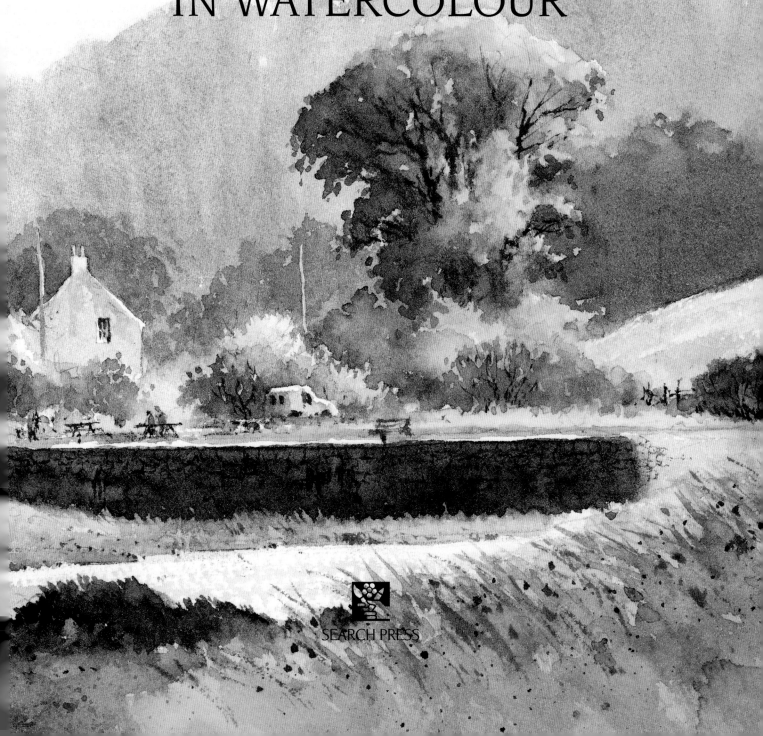

SEARCH PRESS

First published in Great Britain 2020

Uses material from *David Bellamy's Winter Landscapes in Watercolour* by Search Press, 2014

Search Press Limited
Wellwood, North Farm Road,
Tunbridge Wells, Kent TN2 3DR

Reprinted 2021

ISBN: 978-1-78221-899-9

The Publishers and author can accept no
responsibility for any consequences arising from
the information, advice or instructions given in
this publication.

Suppliers
If you have difficulty in obtaining any of the
materials and equipment mentioned in this book,
then please visit the Search Press website for
details of suppliers: www.searchpress.com

Publisher's note
All the step-by-step photographs in this book
feature the author, David Bellamy, demonstrating
his watercolour painting techniques. No models
have been used.

You are invited to visit the author's website
and blog:

www.davidbellamy.co.uk

http://davidbellamyart.blogspot.com

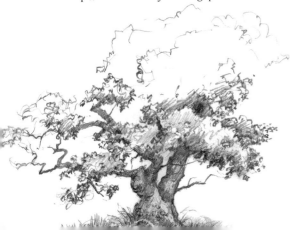

Acknowledgements

*I am indebted to Jenny Keal for checking my
manuscript, Sophie Kersey for editing and making
sense of my writing, and all at Search Press who
do a marvellous job in producing such great results,
and are a pleasure to work with.*

*APV Films have produced two practical DVDs
related to my painting of the seasons:
Summer Landscapes in Watercolour and
Winter Landscapes in Watercolour.
These are available from the author's website:
www.davidbellamy.co.uk or from APV Films:
www.apvfilms.com.*

Front cover
Penberry Hill
16.5 x 24cm (6½ x 9½in)
This painting is shown in full on page 17.

Page 1
Brecon-Abergavenny Canal
25.4 x 33cm (10 x 13in), 425gsm (200lb) Not paper
This painting is also shown on page 40.

Pages 2–3
Cresswell Quay
23 x 30.5cm (9 x 12in)
This painting is also shown on page 28.

These pages
Farm, Staffordshire Moors
22.8 x 38cm (9 x 15in)
The sketch for this painting appears at the top of page 51.

Contents

INTRODUCTION 6

MATERIALS 8

BASIC BRUSH
TECHNIQUES 12

SUMMER 14
LAKELAND WATERFALL 20
MOOR IN SUMMER 30

AUTUMN 36
AUTUMN WATERFALL 42

WINTER 48
WINTER MOUNTAINS 56
FARM IN SNOW 71

SPRING 78
AFTER THE SPRING SHOWER 82

PLANNING PAINTINGS 88

FURTHER TECHNIQUES 92

INDEX 96

Introduction

Living in the UK, we landscape artists are blessed not only with a wide variety of landscapes, but with changing seasons which add further variation to those landscapes. One of the joys of the outdoor artist is visiting the same scene at different times of year and finding that that dramatic snow-bound mountain is now a rich green bathed in sunlight. While summer days can make for pleasurable outings into the countryside in search of landscapes to paint, many artists find it a difficult time of year with all that overwhelming greenery, and often superb subjects are hidden behind massed foliage or riotous vegetation. In the following pages I will try to help you overcome these irritations and make the most of the warmer days.

During winter, these problems vanish: there is normally a greater variety of colour and winter trees take on a different, at times romantic, beauty in their naked splendour. Winter light is strikingly different from that of summer, giving the artist more opportunities for dramatic mood and heightened accentuation of a motif. Landscapes completely transformed under snow offer an excellent opportunity to study the reflections of light and colour. The landscape environment is one of enormous complexity, and deep snow goes a long way to simplify this complex subject for us.

Working outdoors in the coldest weather has never been universally popular. Of the French Impressionists, who took great pains to work directly from nature, only Monet, Pissarro and Sisley did any substantial work in the snow. Monet in particular was a hardy soul who painted outdoors in the harshest of winters, and was sometimes spotted working at his easel in deep snow, clothed in three overcoats and gloves, with a heater at his feet. We now have far more efficient winter clothing and aids to working outdoors in less than ideal weather, but I'm not suggesting that you subject yourself to the bleakest conditions in which to paint or sketch. There are now easier ways of capturing the coldest of winter scenes than following Monsieur Monet's example.

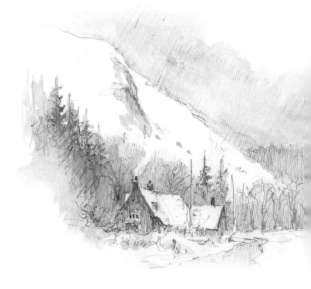

Elan village under snow

6

This book aims to take you from painting the hot summer days, through the misty and colourful scenery of autumn, to making the most of winter when all is laid bare, and on into the snow-covered countryside with its landscapes of quiet beauty and new challenges. Finally there is a section on springtime with its promise of longer days and fresh colours. The seasons, both in topographical detail and weather effects, can at times merge into each other, to give us even in winter some truly delightful warm, sunny moods amidst raw, snow-bound landscapes, making it an absolute joy to be out recording the scenes in sketch or photographic form. I shall show you how to capture these moments, making full use of the lighting – for sometimes the scene is more about atmosphere and lighting than about a topographical feature – and how to respond to the original material in your painting at home.

After writing the *Winter Landscapes* book, I was often asked if I would be doing one on summer landscapes. I decided the best response was to extend the *Winter Landscapes* book, with its sections on late autumn and spring, into an all-seasons one. While this book still contains most of the material from *Winter Landscapes* – winter being so varied that I feel it needs to be the most prominent – there is also a wealth of material on the summer countryside. Whether you can't wait to get out sketching in wild snow flurries, prefer to paint while picnicking in a summer meadow, or choose to paint autumn scenes from the comfort of your home, you should find much to inspire and help you in the following pages.

An Cearcallach, Scottish Highlands
30.5 x 38cm (12 x 15in), 640gsm (300lb) Rough paper

In this Highland scene, sunlight enhances the warm late autumn colours and evening mist adds a hint of mystery to the background. The summer midges have gone, the air is still, and the gentle evening sunlight makes it a pleasure to be out painting as winter approaches.

The yellow-orange tints were achieved with various mixtures of gamboge and cadmium orange and the wine-red massed birch twigs with permanent alizarin crimson. The foreground was accentuated with light red. This is a time when you can happily run riot with your reds.

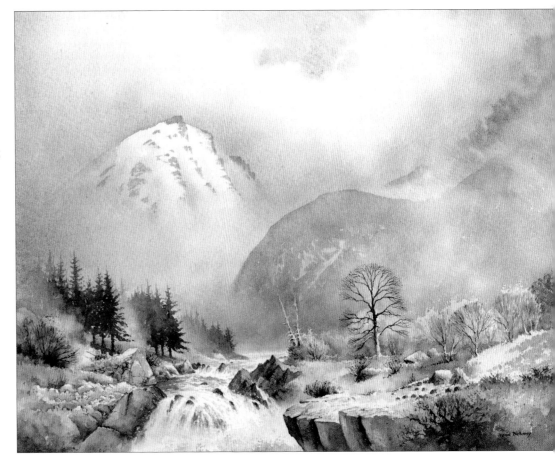

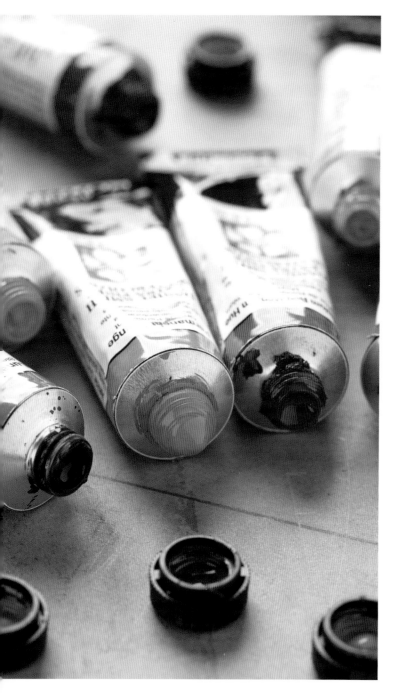

Materials

Paints

Watercolour paints are available in tubes, pans and half-pans. I normally use half-pans for outdoor sketching, supplemented with tube colours on expedition or travel abroad. For the larger studio paintings, tube colours are essential, as one can quickly mix large washes. Choice of colours is up to the individual. I always work with artists' quality paints as they are more powerful and finely ground, but the students' variety are cheaper and there is not a great difference in quality with many colours.

If you are new to painting, start with a few colours and get to know them before adding more. My basic colours are: French ultramarine, burnt umber, cadmium yellow pale, cadmium red, cobalt blue, Winsor blue or phthalo blue, alizarin crimson or quinacridone red, new gamboge, light red and yellow ochre, plus white gouache for minor highlights. Add the following colours when you feel confident, but preferably not all at once: burnt sienna, raw umber, aureolin, viridian, indigo, cerulean blue, Naples yellow, cadmium orange, raw sienna and vermilion.

I now use the Daniel Smith Extra Fine range of watercolours. I love their wide range of granulating colours, as well as some of the new spectacular pigments. Colours that I particularly like and have used in some of the demonstrations in this book are: transparent red oxide, sodalite genuine, zoisite genuine, Aussie red gold, green apatite genuine, nickel titanate yellow and lunar blue. Always study the manufacturers' labels and leaflets and avoid any fugitive colours. These will also tell you if the colour is transparent, opaque or falls between the two, whether it granulates, and the degree of staining.

I sometimes use Daniel Smith watercolour ground to create textured effects in foregrounds (see page 29).

If you are not using Daniel Smith colours, you can approximate the colours as follows:

- Nickel titanate yellow: Naples yellow.
- Sodalite genuine: a mixture of burnt umber and French ultramarine (note that sodalite genuine induces much stronger granulation).
- Green apatite genuine: French ultramarine mixed with cadmium yellow pale for light greens; and raw sienna or yellow ochre for duller greens.
- Transparent red oxide: light red.
- Aussie red gold: cadmium orange, but this is more opaque and not quite so vibrant.
- Lunar blue: this is really quite unique, with strong granulations that can vary unpredictably, and often in a delightful way. There is no simple replacement.

Paper and sketchbooks

Watercolour paper is best bought in imperial-sized sheets, which are cheaper and can be cut to whatever size and configuration you wish. Pads, and blocks that are glued all round the four edges so that you don't have to stretch the paper, are good for working away from home. Usually the paper comes in weights of 190gsm (90lb), 300gsm (140lb), 425gsm (200lb) or 640gsm (300lb), with some manufacturers having a more extended range. The 640gsm (300lb) paper is as thick as cardboard; the 190gsm (90lb) version rather flimsy and prone to cockling. The 300gsm (140lb) paper will most likely need stretching before painting unless you work on really small sizes, so many people find the 425gsm (200lb) paper the ideal weight, as it does not need stretching unless you are painting larger works, and it is less expensive than the 640gsm (300lb) type.

Most papers come in three types of surface: Rough, Hot Pressed (smooth) and Not (or Cold Pressed). Hot Pressed paper is excellent for fine detail, but you may find it best to leave this surface until you are more experienced, as it dries rather more quickly. A Rough surface is extremely effective for creating textures or ragged edges, or for laying a broken wash with the dry-brush technique, although it is not best for fine detail. The most popular paper is the Not surface, which falls between the other two types in degree of smoothness.

Buy a few sheets from different manufacturers to test which suits you best. Most of the paintings in this book were done on Saunders Waterford paper.

Granulations

This is an example of how lunar blue granulates, creating speckles of darker colour in the hollows of the paper. This has been done on Waterford Not paper, but if you use a Rough surface, the granulation is even more pronounced.

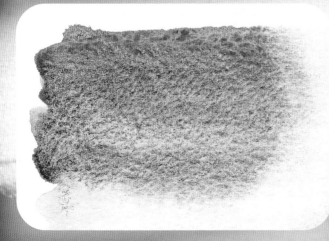

Brushes

The finest brushes for watercolour are undoubtedly sable, though there are excellent synthetic brushes on the market. Kolinsky sable brushes have a fine tip, a large belly to hold copious amounts of paint, and the ability to spring back into shape and not lie limp after one brush stroke. A good compromise, if you find sables too expensive, is to buy a brush of mixed sable and synthetic hairs. Large squirrel-hair mops make lovely wash brushes, although they are prone to losing the odd hair now and then.

The minimum brushes would be a large squirrel mop for washes, a no. 7 or 8 round, a no. 4 round, a no. 1 rigger and a 13mm (½in) flat brush. Add a no. 10 or 12 round and a no. 6 round when you feel the need and you are well set up. More specialized brushes for certain applications, such as a fan brush, can also help on occasion, but are not essential. Take care of your brushes and they will last well. Wash them out with clean water after use.

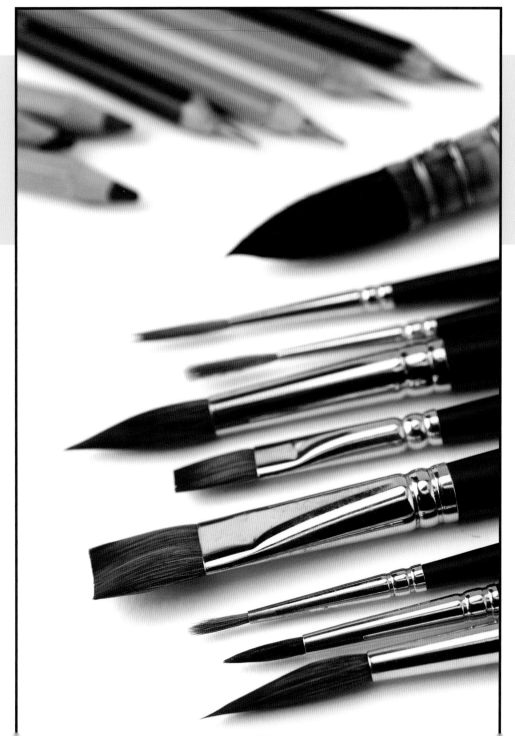

Some of the brushes used in the step-by-step demonstrations in this book, from front to back: a no. 7, no. 4 and no. 1 round (no.s 8 and 6 were also used), a 13mm (½in) flat, a 6mm (¼in) flat, a no. 10 round and a no. 2 and no. 1 rigger, with a squirrel mop.

Other materials

At least one drawing board, a selection of pencils from 2B to 4B, a putty eraser, a soft sponge, at least one large water pot, masking fluid and a scalpel are all essential items. Also useful are bulldog clips, an old toothbrush for spattering, tissues and rags. I find a plant spray is useful to speed up the mixing of colours accurately, and occasionally for spraying over a damp wash to create a speckled effect. If you intend stretching paper, then a roll of gummed tape will be required.

You will need a large palette on which you can lay out the colours you are using, many of which will be for small areas of detail, and some for slightly larger areas. A palette with deep wells is needed for mixing up pools of colour for the main washes. Many artists prefer to use a saucer, butchers' tray or large plate, and so long as it is white and does not affect the way you see the colours, this is perfectly fine. For a large wash, the whole saucer would be needed, but for small detail, many mixes can take place on one dinner plate.

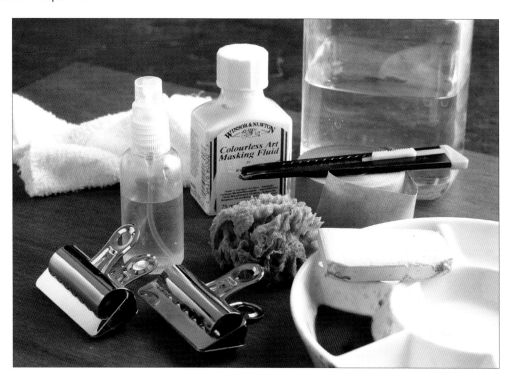

Sketching outdoors

If you are tentative about sketching outdoors, then start with a minimal kit (shown right) of an A5 cartridge pad, a couple of graphite water-soluble pencils and a water brush, which contains its own water supply in the handle. This enables you to work quickly, wet or dry, without fuss. Try working with this, and when you gain confidence, add a small box of watercolours in half-pans, a few brushes and a water pot. Most watercolour boxes include an integral palette in the lid. I sometimes use Derwent Inktense blocks, water-soluble ink blocks, for sketching. Cartridge paper can be difficult to work on with watercolours until you are used to it, so you might prefer a small book of watercolour paper. All this is stored in a belt bag, with gloves to keep out the cold. Later you can expand this kit to suit your needs. I also carry larger sketchbooks and additional materials in a rucksack.

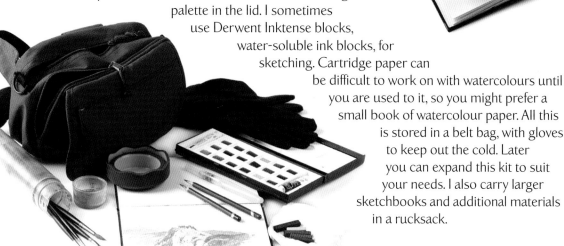

Basic brush techniques

How you handle your brush is critical to the success of your painting, and time spent practising various brush techniques will be well rewarded. For some techniques, such as creating texture with the side of the brush, or the stabbing technique, for example, you can happily use an old, worn brush – in fact it makes sense to do so, as you don't want to wear out those marvellous new, well-pointed sables too quickly – while for delicate, detailed work, you need to reserve your best brushes and keep them in good order. I also use an old, large brush for mixing colours. In this section we look at a few basic techniques on how to achieve certain effects with your brushes.

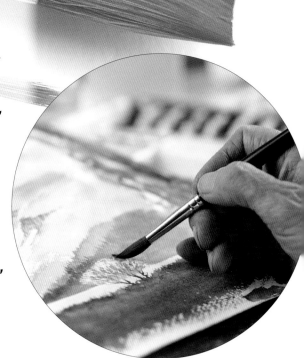

Stabbing method

This is extremely useful for suggesting masses of twigs with a few strokes. Simply stab the brush down onto the paper at the point where you want the extremity of the twigs to start, and then drag it towards the centre of the bush or tree. Doing it this way gives an energetic effect. Practise it on scrap paper first to ensure the brush contains the right consistency of paint. The left-hand example was done with a no. 4 round brush, the right-hand pair with a 6mm (¼in) flat brush.

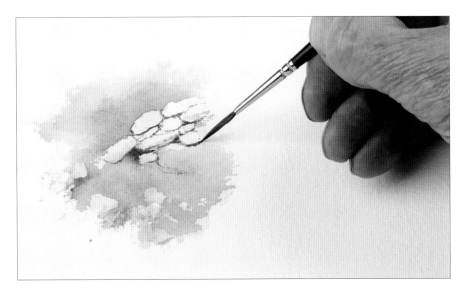

Varying marks and lines with a rigger

By putting varying pressure on a brush, you can create more interesting marks and lines, as in this section of a dry-stone wall painted with a fine rigger brush.

Creating textures with the side of a brush

With this technique, the brush is dragged across the paper on its side, diagonally in this case, where a rough mountain slope is descending to a lake. By testing the effect on spare paper, you can assess how liquid to make the mixture. On Rough paper, this method is extremely effective in creating broken washes, but it still works well on a Not surface. It is hard to beat when you need rough or broken texture, sparkle on water or boulder scree tumbling down below a crag.

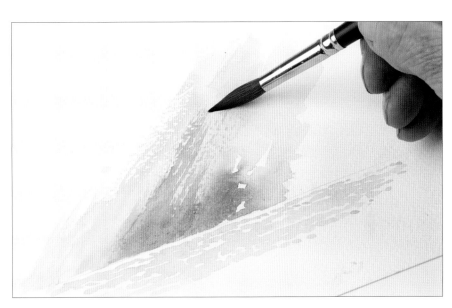

Flat brushes for lifting out paint

Flat brushes are extremely effective for lifting out paint when brushed sideways as shown. It is fairly easy to create light tree trunks in this way without having the chore of working round the tree shapes with a dark wash in a negative fashion. They are also useful for removing unwanted paint. For this type of technique, you need to ensure the brush is one of the thinner flats, as this will ensure more delicate results.

Summer

Warm summer days are when the majority of landscape artists enjoy getting outside to seek those subjects that inspire their work, whether they are capturing them in sketches or photographs. Strong sunlight can bring the landscape to life, and many subjects that we might well ignore during the rest of the year are suddenly infused with a much more exciting combination of light and shadow. In this section you will learn how to accentuate this sense of sunlight in your paintings, engendering a feeling of summer warmth and brightening up your foregrounds with wild flowers and rampant undergrowth. You will also learn how to cope with all those overwhelming greens. Be aware, though, that there are exciting possibilities when the weather is a little bit on the moody side, and these often produce the best paintings.

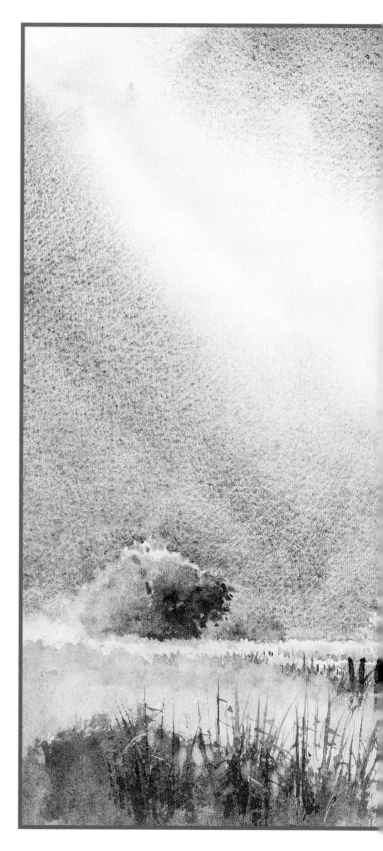

Moody Fen
23 x 35.5cm (9 x 14in), 425gsm (200lb) Rough paper

I came across this scene in Cambridgeshire fenland on a moody August afternoon, with its understated greens and grey sky – and there's a lot of sky in Cambridgeshire, with no mountains to get in the way. Although I haven't included much by way of detail in the sky, the sheer power of the granulation effects of the sodalite genuine mixed with lunar blue more than makes up for this, without detracting from the composition. The light diagonal stretch of Naples yellow relieves the overall gloom of the sky. Aussie red gold on the boathouse roof adds a striking spot of colour. Often you come across features festering in drab colours, so it's worth considering a splash of bright colour at such times. For the detail in the reeds massing along the right-hand bank, I used two methods to achieve depth. Firstly I laid on medium green with green apatite genuine, then when this was dry, I detailed in the reeds, working negatively by painting the dark gaps with the green plus lunar blue, thus highlighting the lighter stalks of the reeds. When this was all dry, I rendered the lightest reeds with white gouache tinged with some nickel titanate yellow.

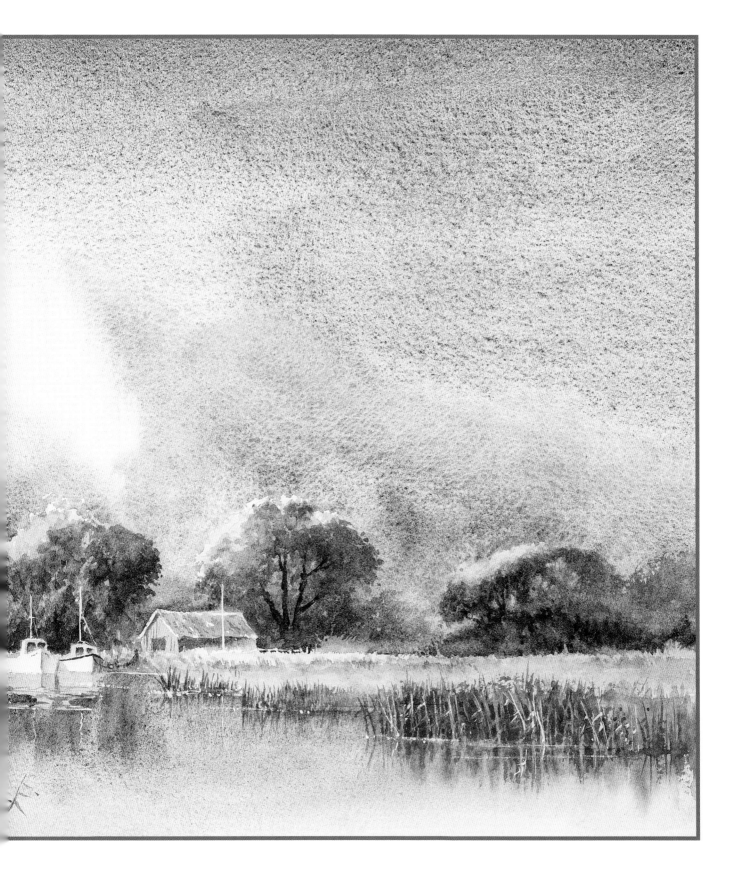

Managing summer greens

Many summer scenes are dominated by greens of many shades, often to an overwhelming degree, and this becomes quite a challenge to the artist. Do you wish to record every nuance of green exactly as it stands, or maybe paint the same amount of greenery but use fewer greens? Or should you make changes to suit yourself, either reducing the amount of green or completely changing to other colours? The first option is laborious and unlikely to produce an interesting result. Trying to render the scene exactly as it is usually stifles creativity. You need to inject something of yourself into the work, and the other two options offer more excitement and interest. On these two pages you will see a variety of approaches.

Cottages Near St Davids
22.3 x 29cm (8¾ x 11½in), 640gsm (300lb) Not paper

If you wish to reduce the effect of overwhelming greenery, you can simply avoid using any green in the distance. In this scene, the area beyond the buildings has been painted in yellow, reds and greys, with the red toned down to suggest distance. I have further reduced the green cover in the foreground by breaking it up with boulders, flowers and patches of strong red. Although these features were actually present, if you wish to diminish the green effect, you can introduce similar objects such as rocks, stones, puddles, patches of gravel, a wide track or whatever might fit into the composition, but try not to overwork the area. Bringing in cut fields not only reduces the impact of the greenery, but also introduces a pleasing variety in the landscape.

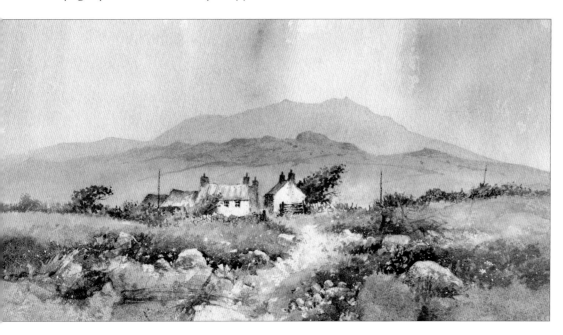

Mixing summer greens

The spring greens chart on page 80 shows some excellent examples for early summer, but for lovely warm greens, mixtures of cadmium yellow pale with French ultramarine, cobalt blue or indigo will extend your range. Substitute cadmium yellow pale with gamboge for even warmer mixes. Adding a touch of red such as cadmium red into these mixtures will give you even more possibilities. I admit that green apatite genuine has become a favourite for me with its rich colour and strong granulations that suggest foliage without me having to do too much work.

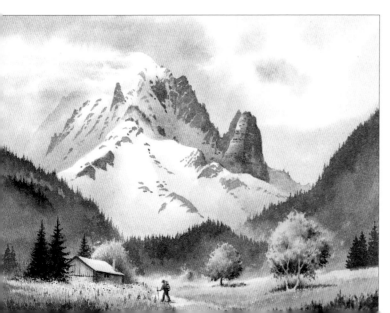

Alpine Meadow
23 x 33cm (9 x 13in), 300gsm (140lb) Not paper

Using strong tonal contrasts is an effective way of suggesting sunshine. Summer Alpine meadows, resplendent with wild flowers, make excellent foregrounds to the snow-capped distant peaks. There are a number of greens in this painting ranging from almost pure yellow to extremely dark greens. The dark conifers and foreground shadows, together with the cast shadows under the trees, help to emphasize the feeling of sunlight in the lighter parts of the meadow. For the cooler greens on the light trees, I used cadmium yellow pale with cobalt blue, but for much of the warmer grassy foreground, I applied gamboge.

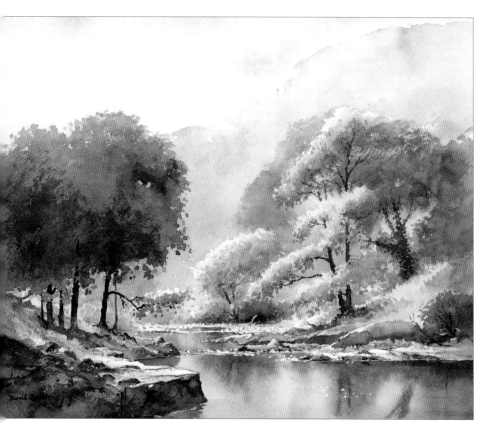

River Mellte

21.5 x 26cm (8½ x 10¼in), 300gsm (140lb)
Not paper

Here we look at creating depth with greens. The greens here are in three degrees of colour temperature. In order to suggest distance, the background ones are blue-green, a mixture of cobalt blue and yellow ochre. This wash is quite weak for the furthest bank of trees rising up the side of the gorge, but much stronger for the darker foliage just right of centre above and to the left of the tall, sunlit trees. The small tree in the centre is slightly greener: cobalt blue and cadmium yellow pale with more yellow in the mix, while the closer trees on both sides were painted with French ultramarine and cadmium yellow pale, with raw umber and ultramarine for the darker shadows. This gives a sense of depth and space and the overall impact of the massed greens is lessened. The lack of detail in the furthest mass of trees also helps to suggest distance. For the water I began with a fluid wash of cobalt blue with some yellow ochre touched in, and then dropped in wet-into-wet: cadmium yellow pale for the lighter reflections and French ultramarine with raw umber for the darks.

Penberry Hill

16.5 x 24cm (6½ x 9½in)

I sketched this in early summer when the greens were much in evidence on the hill, but here I have brought the warmer colours further down the hillside and reduced the foreground greens with flowers and patches of red. The middle section was pretty much colour-faithful with a sort of faded green. I left out a caravan and electricity poles and added in chickens.

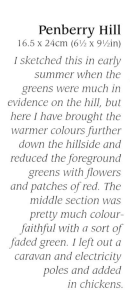

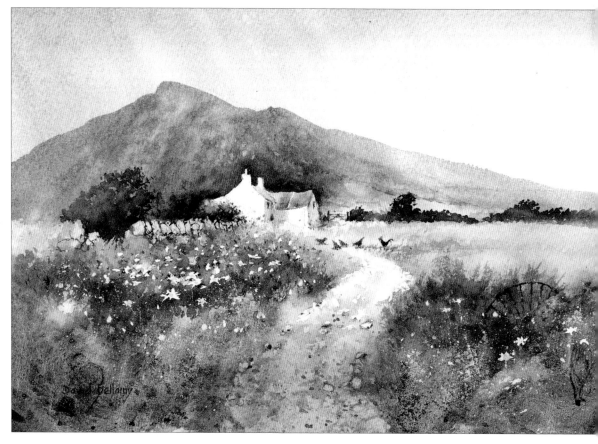

17

Painting summer trees

One of the most common failures in painting summer trees is to create what look like lumps of green dough stuck on a matchstick. This is easy to avoid as shown in the examples. Try to find trees where the trunk and several main branches are visible, as these give shape and character. If you can't see any branches, introduce two or three. Trunks and branches often appear as dark silhouettes, but it gives the tree more life if you add colour while the limb is still wet. Reds, pinks, yellows and greens work, and sometimes I even drop a touch of phthalo blue into the dark trunk.

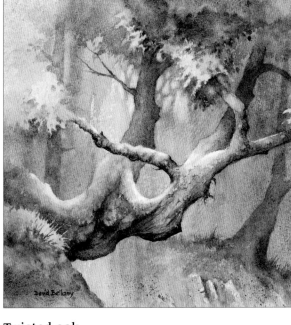

Twisted oak
20.3 x 20.3cm (8 x 8in), 300gsm (140lb) Not paper

Many oak trees look ungainly and awkward, but a lovely mature oak, contorted and with a weathered, textured trunk, can be a gem for the artist. This one grew horizontally out of a bank, then curved upwards, its branches breaking up the strong lines of other trunks and branches. I have simplified the tree by leaving out several less interesting branches: don't hesitate to cut out those that don't suit your purpose. Mosses and lichens gave way in places to naked bark, creating varied colouring. Much of the background was created wet-into-wet, sometimes painting only part of a trunk to enhance a sense of mystery. The wet-into-wet technique is excellent for woodland backgrounds. The composition is overwhelmingly green, painted in the main with a mixture of viridian and bloodstone genuine, with cadmium yellow pale in places. The intense rich greens at the top and the bottom left were painted in green apatite genuine.

Losing branches into shadow areas gives a natural appearance

Blobs of light gouache help suggest lighter foliage

A sharply defined feature such as a stile helps to counter amorphous foliage areas

Branches and stalks painted negatively provide variation

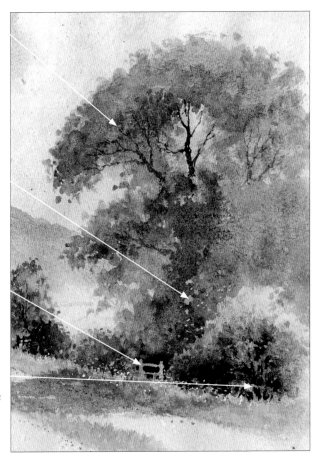

Mature tree in full leaf

You often cannot see any trunks or branches in trees with dense foliage, and in this case I tend to add my own to give the tree shape. Small blobs to suggest leaves placed just outside the boundary of the main foliage ensure your trees won't look like lumps of dough, and here I've also blobbed in a few in light green gouache near the stile.

Beech tree sketch

Sometimes I sketch lone trees where I find good examples, as these can be inserted into a painting. This was sketched as spring was turning into summer, a rewarding time for studying mature trees as you can still view the branches and trunks among the foliage. I love the way sunlight throws the cast shadows of branches across the trunks. These were rendered wet-into-wet on the right-hand trunk and wet-on-dry on the left, to compare.

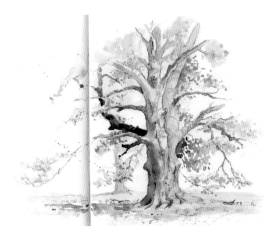

Birch tree

Birches are distinctive, beautiful trees that can enhance a landscape whether as the centre of interest or as a supporting feature. Sketch and photograph good specimens as these can be added to a composition as required. The following two stages will give you an idea of how to tackle them.

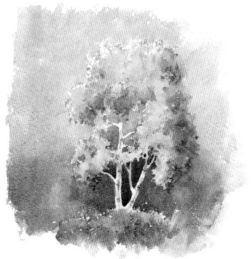

Birch tree stage 1

I drew the outline with a 4B pencil, then applied green apatite genuine with cadmium yellow pale.

Birch tree final stage

First I wetted the trunks with clean water, then I dragged transparent red oxide down the centres of the trunks, creating a soft effect. A few drops of lunar blue were added here and there. Next I painted a mixture of French ultramarine and cadmium red around the trunks and branches to highlight them light against dark. I added shadows where the trunks go under the foliage and spotted dark flecks of French ultramarine and burnt umber into the trunks in places. The sketch was finished with white gouache spatter.

Using the side of the brush for foliage

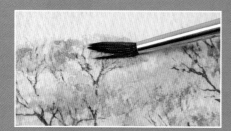

The brush should not be too wet for this technique. Holding it on its side, drag the belly of the brush downwards over the paper to create textured clumps of foliage.

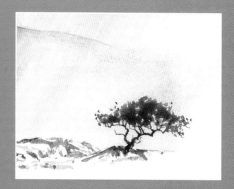

Spotting individual leaves

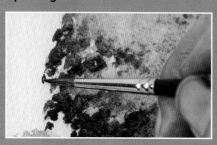

Using a small brush, dab on individual leaves or clumps beyond the main mass of the tree. This helps to create a much more realistic effect.

Thorn tree

With their twisted, angular limbs, thorn trees make a beautiful addition to a mountain or moorland environment, or even to a pastoral landscape. Seek out good examples to add to your compositions at all times of the year.

LAKELAND WATERFALL

Masses of foliage from many trees can create confusion, so here I show how using a combination of misty effects and strong granulating colour can simplify this natural chaos. Often with background mist like this, I hint at wet-into-wet tree shapes in the background, but here I've kept it simple with green apatite genuine. If you don't have this colour, mix French ultramarine and cadmium yellow pale, working a darker colour such as raw umber into the ultramarine where you want a darker area.

Materials used

Saunders Waterford 640gsm (300lb) Rough watercolour paper
Brushes: Squirrel mop, no. 8, no. 6 and no. 10 round, rigger, 13mm (½in) flat
Colours: Green apatite genuine, cadmium yellow medium hue, alizarin crimson, yellow ochre, cobalt blue, burnt umber, French ultramarine, zoisite genuine, transparent red oxide, nickel titanate yellow, Aussie red gold, sodalite genuine
Masking fluid, old brush, 5B pencil
Toothbrush, paper mask, scalpel

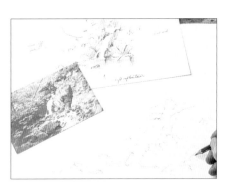

1 Use a 5B pencil to draw the outlines of the scene. I referred to my studio sketch and photograph.

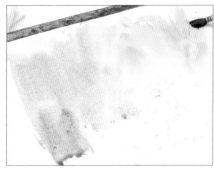

2 Mask some leaves with masking fluid and an old brush. Paint clear water over the background with a squirrel mop, then drop in green apatite genuine, which will granulate, creating textured effects.

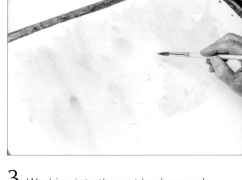

3 Working into the wet background, drop in cadmium yellow medium hue on either side, then use a no. 8 round brush to drop in alizarin crimson and yellow ochre in the centre as a base colour for the rocks.

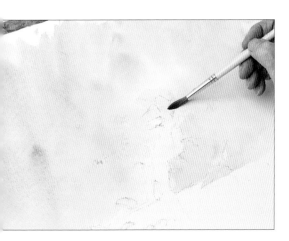

4 Paint a wash of cobalt blue over the distant falling water to make it recede. Fade this out at the top with a damp brush and allow the painting to dry.

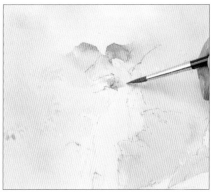

5 Mix burnt umber and French ultramarine to paint rocks at the top of the waterfall. Fade the lower edges. Use the no. 6 round and French ultramarine to hint at falling water.

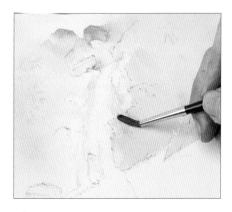

6 With the same mix, drag a dry brush along the edges of the waterfall to suggest rushing water. The dry brush technique creates a speckled effect with the Rough paper.

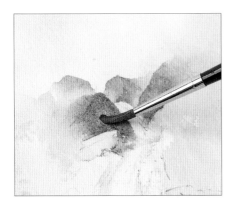

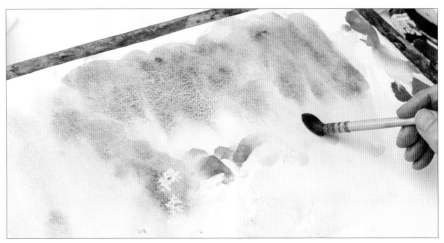

7 Work on the rocks on either side of the waterfall with French ultramarine and burnt umber. Fade off the edges with a damp brush where the rocks enter the water, then drop in yellow ochre to create texture. Allow to dry.

8. Paint over the whole background with a squirrel mop and clean water, then paint on zoisite genuine, which will introduce more granulations as it flows down the paper, creating excellent effects for foliage. Drop cadmium yellow medium hue into the middle ground. Allow to dry naturally.

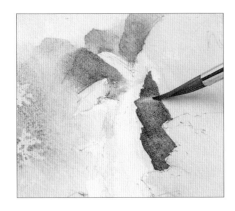

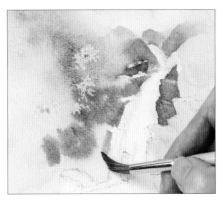

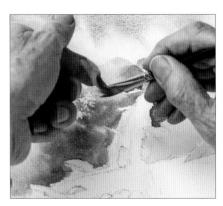

9 Use the no. 8 round brush to paint rocks to the right of the waterfall with French ultramarine and burnt umber. Drop in transparent red oxide while the rocks are wet, then use a damp brush tip to pull out colour where the light catches the rocks.

10 Change to the no. 6 brush to paint detail on the left of the waterfall with French ultramarine and burnt umber. Then use the no. 8 brush to wet the area just below this and drop in the same mix.

11 Pick up nickel titanate yellow on the brush and pull back the bristles to spatter this into this wet brown area. Dot in the same colour wet into wet using the masking fluid brush, then spatter on clean water with an old toothbrush to create a mottled effect.

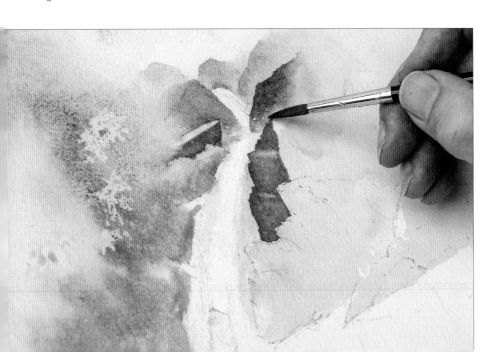

12 Reinforce the falling water with French ultramarine and the dry brush technique, using an old synthetic brush. Leave most of it as white paper. Paint darker rock on the right of the waterfall with a no. 6 brush and burnt umber with French ultramarine, then drop in Aussie red gold wet into wet to bring this rock forwards, creating depth.

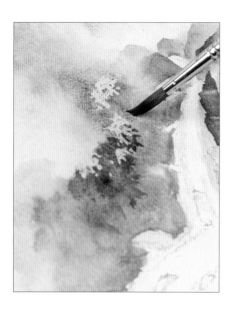

13 Use the no. 8 brush to paint green apatite genuine on the left of the waterfall, around the masked-out foliage.

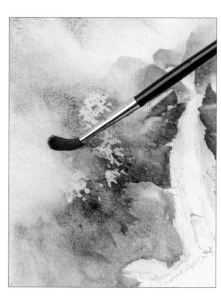

14 Paint rock detail on the left with the no. 6 brush and French ultramarine and burnt umber. Drop in yellow ochre wet into wet and add this colour to the foliage area too.

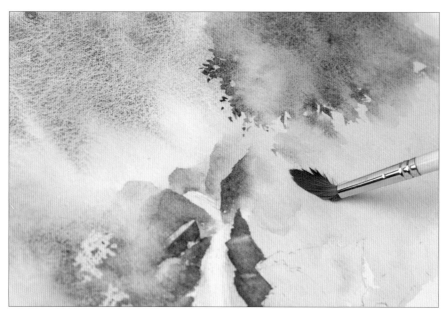

15 Use the squirrel mop to paint green apatite genuine on the right of the painting, then the no. 8 brush to paint foliage detail at the edges of the area. Paint nickel titanate yellow below this area and allow the wet green to run into it.

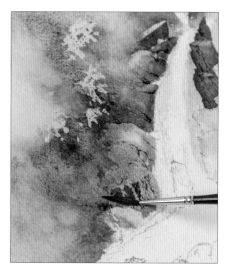

16 With a rigger and sodalite genuine and burnt umber, paint fracture lines in the rocks on both sides of the fall, varying the pressure applied. Use the brush on its side to create texture with dry brushwork.

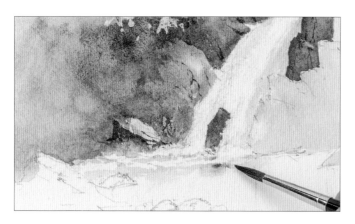

17 Pick up cobalt blue and paint the flat water at the bottom of the waterfall. Use French ultramarine and burnt umber to paint the rock in the middle of the waterfall. Paint the water splashing into the pool with a touch of French ultramarine. Indicate the transition between the foam and the darker pool with French ultramarine, then drop in a reflection with the rock colours wet into wet. Allow the painting to dry.

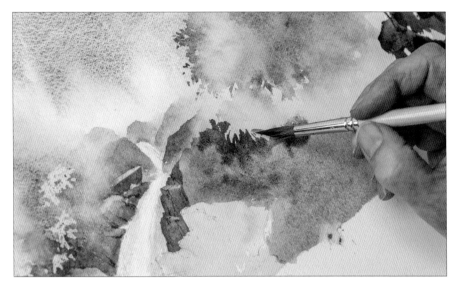

18 Use the no. 8 brush to paint a blue mix of French ultramarine with a little burnt umber to form a contrasting dark area below the light foliage on the right. Drop in yellow ochre wet into wet. Mix sodalite genuine and green apatite genuine and work negatively, painting leaf shapes with the tip of the brush. Lose some edges using a damp brush.

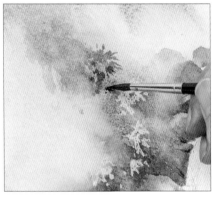

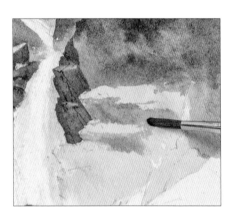

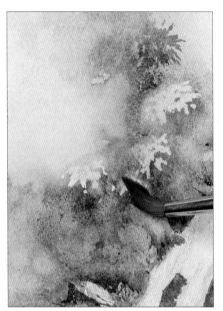

19 Change to a no. 6 brush and paint foliage shapes on the left with the same mix.

20 Make a weak mix of French ultramarine and burnt umber and paint the shadow and detail on the reddish rock to the right of the waterfall. Drop in alizarin crimson wet into wet.

21 Use the same method to model some of the rocks on the left. Rub off the masking fluid in the foliage area. Use a damp 13mm (½in) flat brush to soften some edges, then use a no. 8 brush and cadmium yellow medium hue to colour the previously masked areas. Add green apatite genuine in places. Allow to dry.

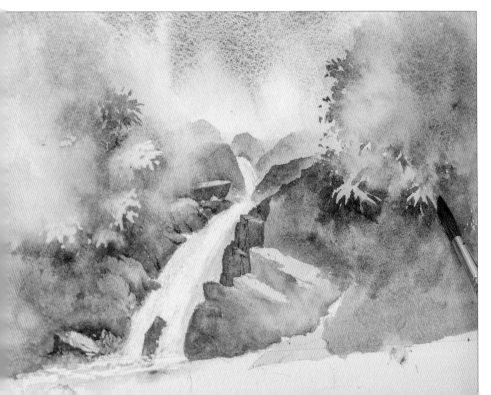

22 On the right of the waterfall, reduce the starkness of the foliage shapes painted negatively with a wash of green apatite genuine.

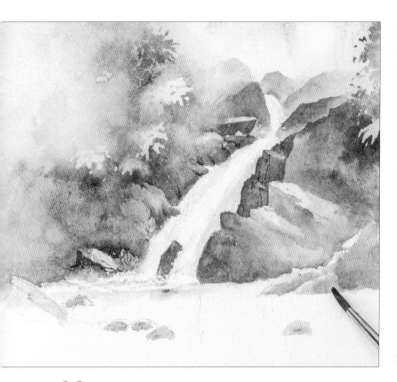

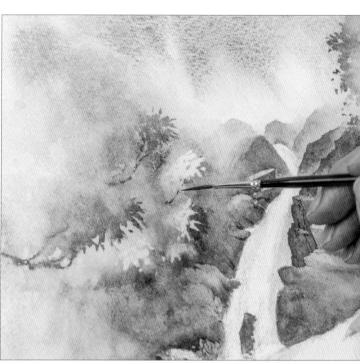

23 Paint the rocks in the stream with the no. 6 brush and a pale mix of French ultramarine and burnt umber. Drop in various colours including yellow ochre and alizarin crimson. Paint the shadow of the rocks at the back of the stream in the same way and drop in Aussie red gold.

24 Work on the foliage on the left with green apatite genuine, then add sodalite genuine to the mix to tighten up and sharpen details. Mix sodalite genuine and burnt umber to paint branches with the rigger.

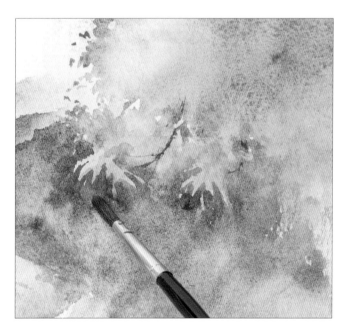

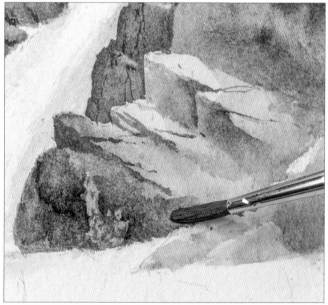

25 Work on the foliage on the left with green apatite genuine, then add sodalite genuine to the mix to tighten up and sharpen details. Mix sodalite genuine and burnt umber to paint branches with the rigger.

26 Work on details in the rock with a mix of sodalite genuine and burnt umber, then paint fracture lines with the rigger. Drop in Aussie red gold with the no. 8 brush.

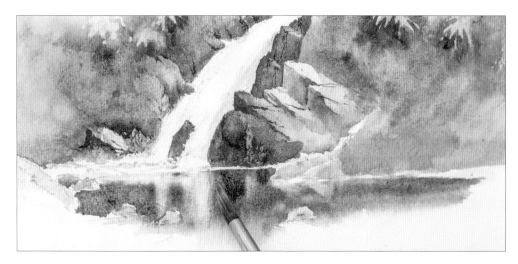

27 Wet the dark area of the pool with clean water, then paint horizontal strokes of burnt umber and French ultramarine. Use a no. 10 brush to drop in touches of colour for reflections: green apatite genuine and sodalite genuine with burnt umber. Work round the light rocks.

28 Paint details on the rocks on the right of the waterfall with the rigger and the same mix, then use the no. 6 brush to paint green apatite genuine to build up the colour of the foliage.

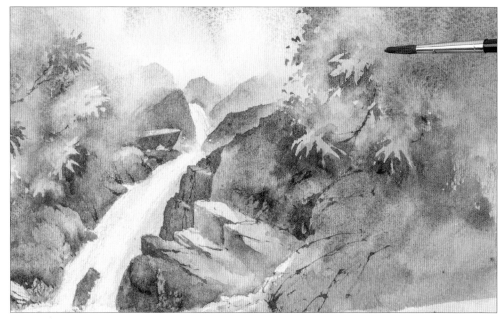

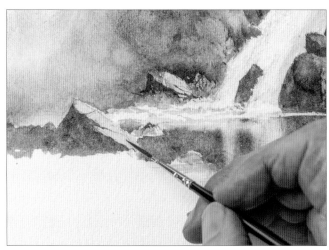

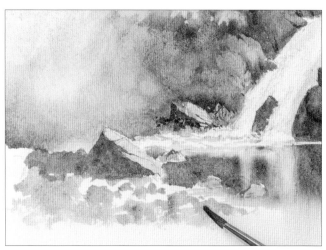

29 Use the rigger with sodalite genuine and burnt umber to paint the rock on the left of the stream. Drop in yellow ochre, then paint the lit side of the rock with alizarin crimson.

30 With the no. 6 brush, paint stones in the stream with French ultramarine and a little burnt umber, then drop in yellow ochre and alizarin crimson to create variety.

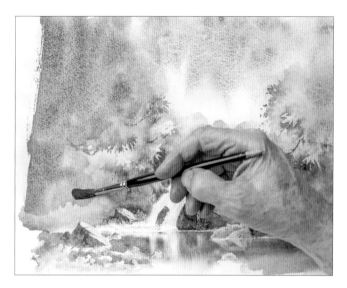

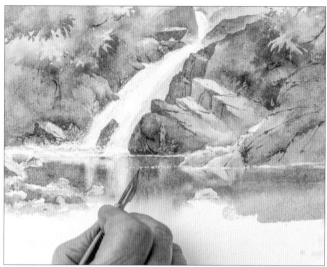

31 Use the rigger with French ultramarine and burnt umber to tighten up details. Use the no. 6 brush to add colour to the left-hand stones. I then assessed the painting within a mount. I decided to extend the dark water to the right by wetting it with a sponge and painting with French ultramarine and burnt umber. I darkened the left-hand foliage with sodalite genuine and green apatite genuine.

32 Use a scalpel to flick out white highlights from the splashing water at the foot of the waterfall, then scratch out horizontal ripples.

The finished painting.

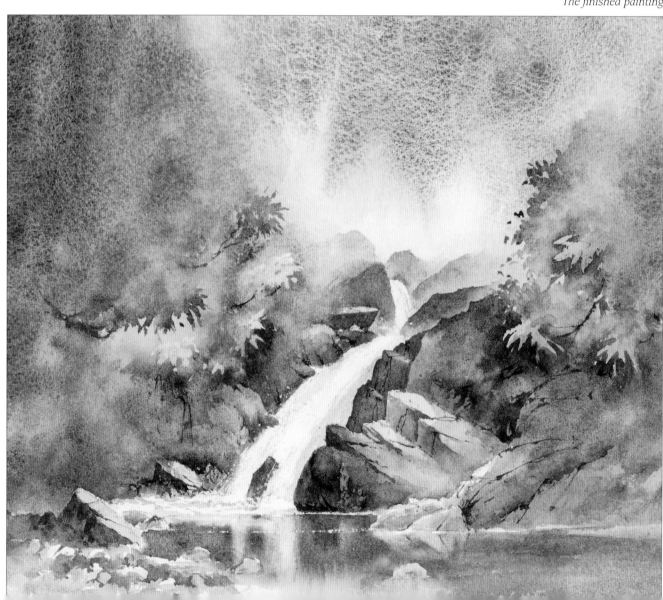

Limited colours for mood

A limited palette creates a feeling of unity, mood and drama. Backlighting will accentuate this. The painting can appear dull if you are using muted colours. Ensuring that you have really strong tonal contrasts, especially around the focal point, will add interest.

River Usk
18 x 24cm (7 x 9½in), 300gsm (140lb) Not paper

The sky was painted with lunar blue and cadmium red, bringing in a touch of nickel titanate yellow down the centre. The misty background hides a lot of distracting detail. I also applied nickel titanate yellow onto the tree masses. The background trees were suggested with lunar blue and cadmium yellow light and the closer ones with green apatite genuine and cadmium yellow light. The shadows were created with lunar blue and green apatite genuine, and the dark trunks and branches with burnt umber and lunar blue. Lunar blue helps create unity in the painting.

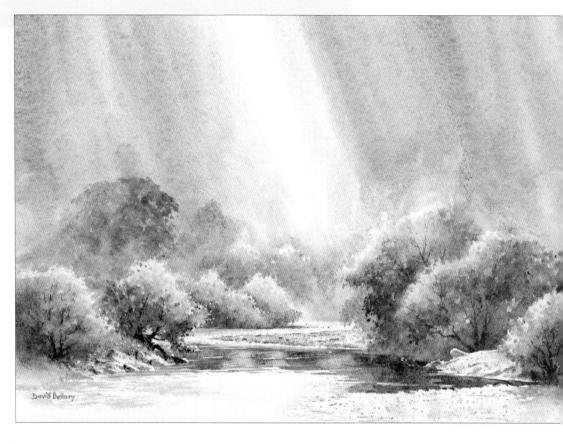

Cottages on the Cliffs
20.3 x 30.5cm (8 x 12in), 640gsm (300lb) Not paper

Here I've used muted colours for mood, but then dropped weak cadmium red into the phthalo blue and yellow ochre background in places. This warms up the landscape without overpowering it. The darker patches are phthalo blue with burnt umber. I used masking fluid on the buildings. For the foreground cliffs, I used weak mixes of yellow ochre and alizarin crimson, with French ultramarine and burnt umber in places.

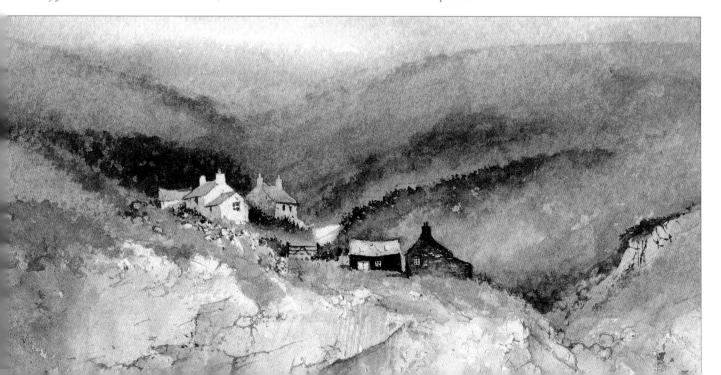

Spot colour and intense light

Sometimes you may wish to create a warm patch of colour around your focal point, and often a spot of colour will suffice to lift a painting and completely change the mood. Don't hesitate to exaggerate the warmth of the colour.

When you want to suggest a scene bathed in brilliant sunshine, reduce detail, as intense light tends to bleach it out. If you include all these effects for creating a sunny subject, it will suggest a hot day. Strong tonal contrasts and cast shadows also enhance this.

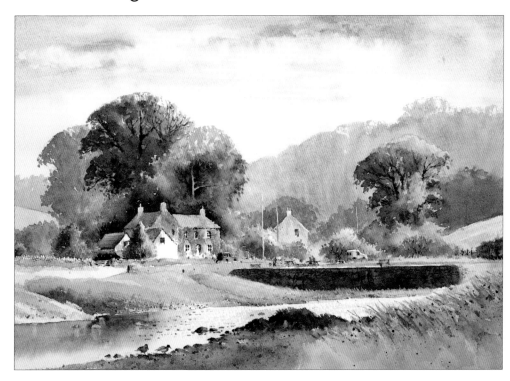

Cresswell Quay
23 x 30.5cm (9 x 12in), 300gsm (140lb) Not paper

Where there is an overwhelming amount of green, it helps to inject a spot of contrasting colour to breathe life into the work. Here the red ivy on the pub does this, particularly as it is a complementary colour to green.

Abinger Hammer

Nestling below the North Downs, this village is a pleasant spot in summer with lush vegetation breaking up the hard lines of the buildings. I began this sketch with a pen drawing on cartridge paper and then applied watercolour, making the bell tower the focal point. To the left of this, I kept the detail and colour low-key to emphasize the tower and right-hand houses. At the bottom of the bell tower, I slightly exaggerated the red, yellow and green patch to emphasize that spot. I kept most of the greens warm, and the strong shadows suggest a hot and sunny summer's day.

Controlled lighting

In the small sketch below, a spot of colour brings the scene to life as evening light hits sandstone crags high on the Sächsische Schweiz in eastern Germany. This 'spotlight' device not only adds interest and life, but also creates a striking focal point in a dramatic scene of sheer faces dropping into dark shadow.

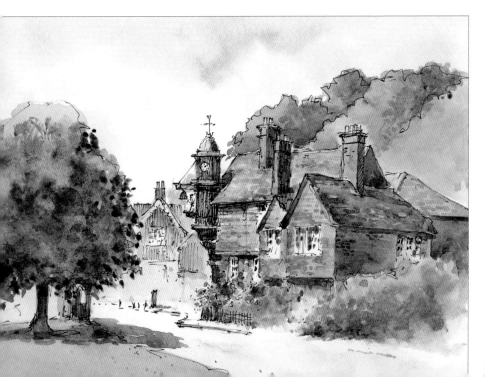

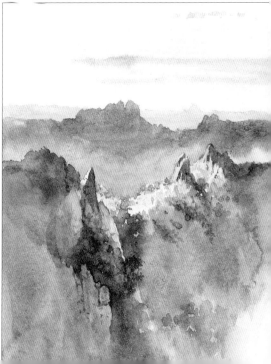

Techniques for summer foregrounds

Foregrounds can be simple, complicated or neutral, and many artists insist on hardly any detail here. However, you may wish to concentrate on the foreground, perhaps using it as your focal point with just a vague stand of trees or building in the distance to suggest the setting. If your middle distance is complicated, keep the foreground simple, perhaps just a plain wash and a hint of detail. You can enhance foregrounds with a puddle, wild flowers, rusting farm machinery in long grass, or whatever catches your imagination. Work these in from sketches and photographs from other scenes.

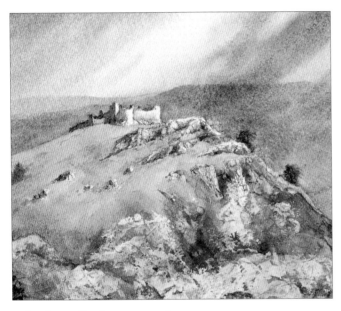

Mixed media foregrounds

Foregrounds are an excellent place to introduce abstract elements or mixed media materials. In this scene I began by sticking a collage of small pieces of tissue-like Oriental papers onto the watercolour paper in the immediate foreground. When these were completely dry, I plastered white Daniel Smith watercolour ground (similar to gesso) over parts of the collage with a painting knife, before allowing the area to dry completely for a day or two. I then painted the scene, with the collage and watercolour ground creating striking textures.

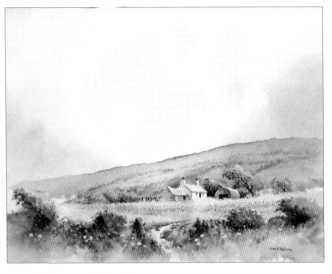

Sunshine and shadows
23 x 30.5cm (9 x 12in) 300gsm (140lb) Not paper

Bringing lush vegetation up to cover walls and other foreground features conveys a lovely sense of summer, and it's also useful for hiding complicated detail. Keep it fairly simple and avoid covering the whole foreground in this way. Here the long grasses obscure much of the dry-stone wall and the flowers punctuate the mass of vegetation to prevent this passage becoming monotonous. Cloud shadow across the foreground helps to highlight the more distant farmhouse and I have added some red in the field: grass is not always green, so try to observe these minute but extremely effective points. Note how the hedgerows on the hillside are muted and intermittent to suggest distance.

Creating stalks and grasses

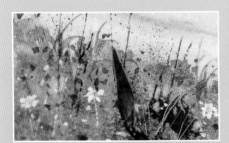

Pick up paint on the edge of a painting knife, test it first on scrap paper, then press the edge onto the painting and drag it vertically down.

Pulling out light grasses in a damp wash

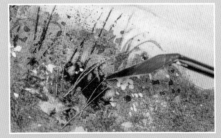

Scratch out lines in damp, dark paint to create lighter stalks and grasses. The tip of the painting knife will not score the paper like a scalpel.

Pulling out colour with a painting knife

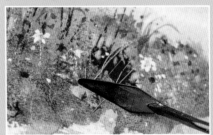

Here the knife is scraped sideways in a damp, dark wash, removing an area of paint to suggest lighter vegetation or stones.

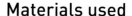

MOOR IN SUMMER

In this demonstration I show a simple approach to a North York Moors scene, with a misty background and weak sunlight falling on the focal point. The majority of buildings in this region have orange-tiled roofs, which I am keen to portray as it illustrates the local character. You may wish to use a lighter weight of paper than the heavy 640gsm (300lb) sheet I have worked on. The composition is based on a pencil sketch I did in an A5 cartridge sketchbook.

Materials used

Saunders Waterford 640gsm (300lb) Rough watercolour paper

Brushes: Squirrel mop, no. 6, no. 1 and no. 8 round, 6mm (¼in) flat, angled flat, rigger

Colours: Sodalite genuine, lunar blue, nickel titanate yellow, yellow ochre, transparent red oxide, cadmium red, green apatite genuine, cadmium yellow medium hue, cobalt blue, French ultramarine, burnt umber, zoisite genuine, Aussie red gold, alizarin crimson, titanium white gouache

Masking fluid, old brush, 5B pencil, wax candle, toothbrush, paper mask, plant spray bottle

Painting knife and scalpel

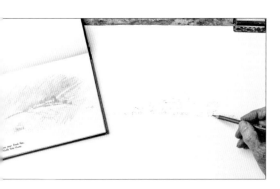

1 Use a 5B pencil to draw the main outlines of the scene. I referred to my field sketch.

2 Mask the roofs, chimneys and windows and the odd fence post using masking fluid applied with an old brush.

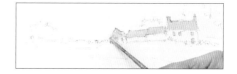

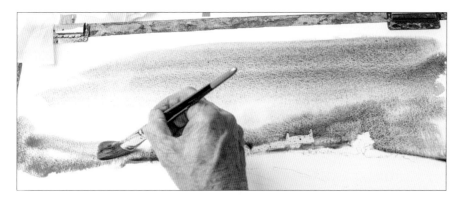

3 Sweep a white wax candle over part of the right side of the moor. The wax catches in the depressions of the Rough paper, creating a speckled resist. Using a squirrel mop, brush clean water over the sky and masked roofs. Paint a wash of sodalite genuine across the sky, leaving a lighter streak, then add lunar blue on the left.

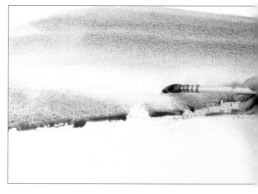

4 Add a touch of nickel titanate yellow to the lighter streak in the sky. Take out any excess water using a barely damp brush, then allow the painting to dry naturally.

5 Wash nickel titanate yellow across the top of the moor area and float in yellow ochre lower down. While this is wet, dab in rogue colours: transparent red oxide, then cadmium red. The paint reveals the texture created by the wax resist.

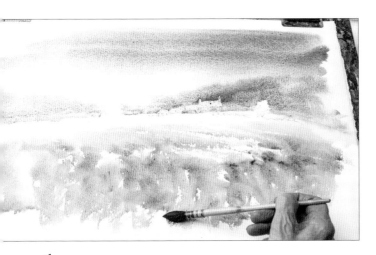
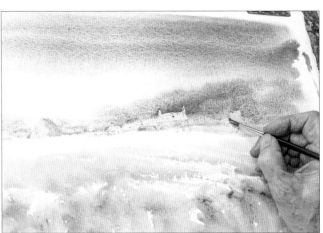

6 Dab green apatite genuine into the area while it is wet. Spray on some clean water from the plant spray bottle to create a speckled texture, then allow to dry naturally.

7 Use the no. 6 brush to paint cadmium yellow medium hue with a touch of green apatite genuine onto the hedgerow in front of the buildings. Paint the trees with the same colour, adding a darker, greener shade to the shadowed sides.

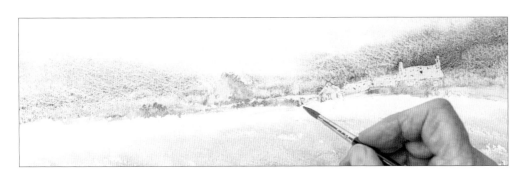

8 Dab touches of the darker green mix into the hedgerow and in front of the house. Drop in a little transparent red oxide in places to vary the effect.

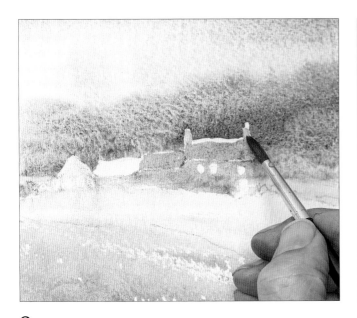
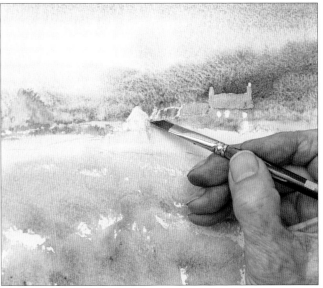

9 When the painting is dry, rub off the masking fluid with a clean finger. Tidy the edges with a damp 6mm (¼in) flat brush. Paint the house roof and chimneys with yellow ochre, then transparent red oxide.

10 Take the angled flat brush and pick up cadmium red on one side and cobalt blue on the other. Separate the hairs and stroke down to create the corrugated iron roof of the building next to the house.

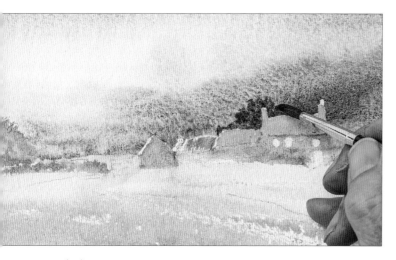 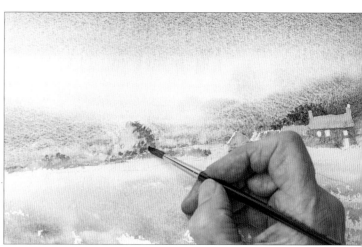

11 With the no. 6 round, paint the building on the far left with a pale mix of French ultramarine and burnt umber, leaving an edge to suggest light catching the roof edge. Drop in yellow ochre wet into wet and allow to dry. Bring out the brightness of the roofs by painting the trees behind with a dark mix of sodalite genuine and zoisite genuine.

12 Paint over the main house again with sodalite genuine and drop in yellow ochre. Shade the right-hand side of the tree with zoisite genuine.

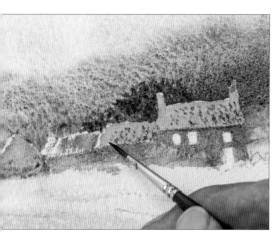

13 Change to the no. 1 brush and paint the chimney pot with Aussie red gold, then add dabs of this and cadmium red to texture the roofs.

14 At this distance it is fine to suggest a five-bar gate with only two-and-a-half bars or so – do this with sodalite genuine.

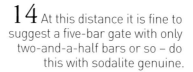

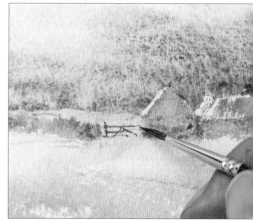

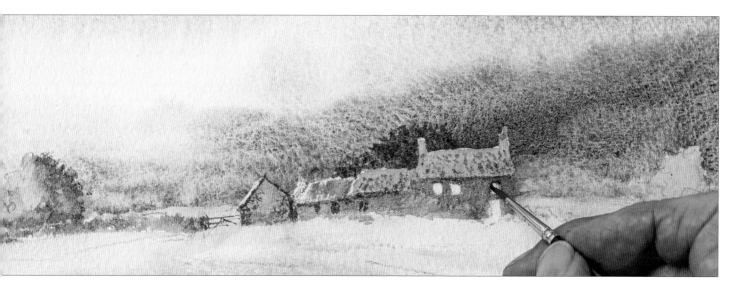

15 Continue adding detail to the buildings with the same brush and mix.

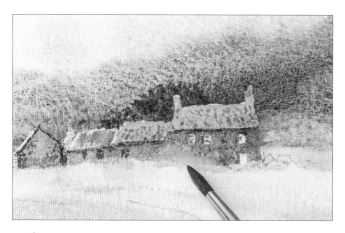

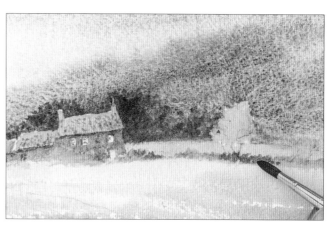

16 At this point I noted that the bush in front of the house didn't stand out well, so I removed some colour with a damp 6mm (¼in) flat brush. Drop in cadmium yellow medium hue with a no. 8 brush.

17 Darken the trees in the background with zoisite genuine to make the roofs stand out. Mix cadmium yellow medium hue with green apatite genuine and vary the height and texture of the hedgerow. Add zoisite genuine to darken some areas such as the shadow under the tree.

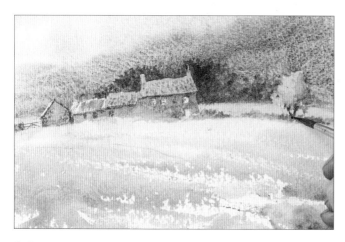

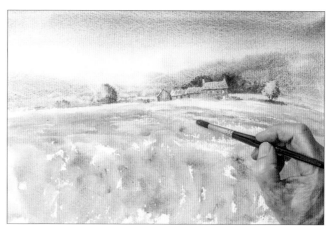

18 Soften the right-hand tree with a damp brush, then paint trunks with sodalite genuine.

19 Work on the moorland with zoisite genuine and green apatite genuine on an old no. 8 brush. Scrub across the Rough paper surface and wax resist to create texture. Add yellow ochre in places. Subdue the texture elsewhere with water for a varied effect.

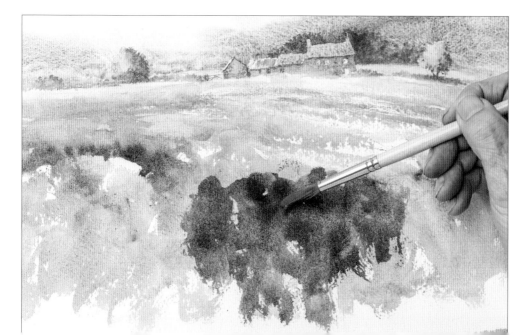

20 Suggest slabs of rock in the foreground by painting negatively around them with zoisite genuine and alizarin crimson.

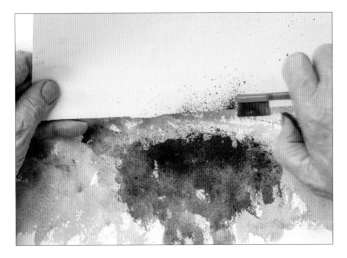

21 Pick up the same mix on an old toothbrush, mask the rest of the painting with scrap paper and spatter the area to add suggestions of small leaves or berries above the red patch.

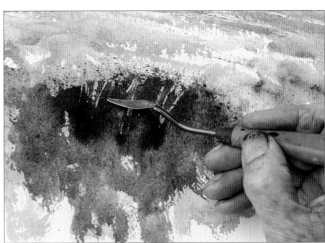

22 Use the point of a painting knife to scratch out more texture.

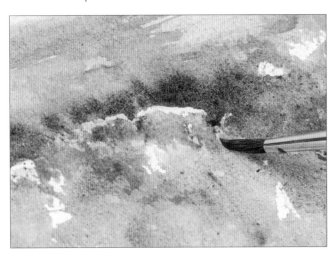

23 Use the no. 6 brush to paint the sides of the rocks you outlined negatively, using French ultramarine and burnt umber and leaving white paper highlights. Drop in yellow ochre, then zoisite genuine wet into wet.

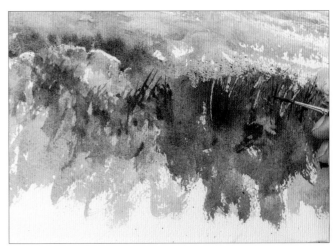

24 Change to a rigger and flick out strokes of the wet colour to create grasses

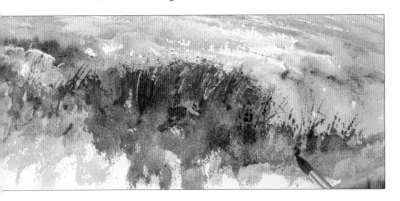

25 Use the tip of the no. 8 brush and zoisite genuine to dot in dark plant shapes in the foreground. Allow to dry.

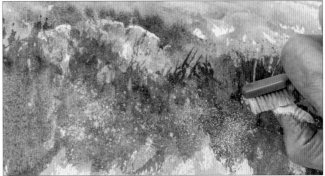

26 Spatter titanium white gouache over both the wet and the dry paint in the foreground, using an old toothbrush. The patchy drying varies the texture achieved.

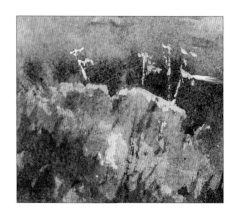 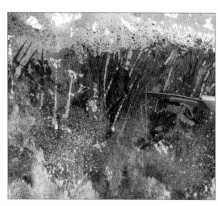 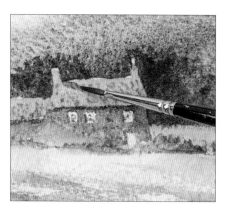

27 Pick up neat titanium white gouache on the tip of the rigger and paint cow parsley stalks on the dark background, then dot in the flowers.

28 Scratch out grasses with the tip of the scalpel.

29 Tidy the windows with the rigger and white gouache. Finally paint a cast shadow from the chimney with zoisite genuine to complete the effect of bright sunlight.

The finished painting.

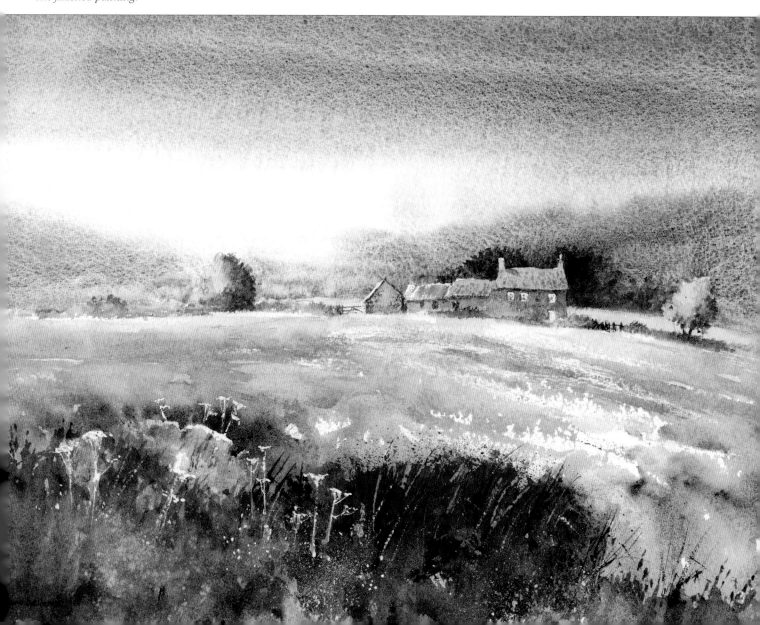

Autumn

As trees shed their leaves, it is a great opportunity for the landscape artist, with all that massed green foliage being replaced by exciting colours and the interesting bare structure of trunks and branches. Early snowfall can sometimes cloak distant hills and mountains, yet vivid autumn colours are still resplendent in the foreground, providing an exciting combination. It really pays to be ready to capture the transient scenes at this time of year with some potential paintings in mind, as gales and storms can quickly change the state of trees in autumn. Certain local trees can put on a spectacular display of colour every year, so watch out for these. Of course, once you have captured these beautiful days, it is fairly easy to transform your original autumn sketches and photographs into a composition with a snowy background, or vice versa. Changing the season in this way can offer you fascinating new possibilities with a favourite subject. In this section we look at these autumn colours which can linger well into the depths of winter. We will also consider some of the lovely atmospheric effects we can encounter at this time of year.

Farm in Autumn Sunlight

23 x 38cm (9 x 15in), Not paper

When you are fed up with an overwhelming prospect of summer greens, it sometimes pays to turn your summer landscape into an autumn one, which is what I have done here. I also often add a little autumnal foliage into my winter scenes, to warm them up. This is easy if you have examples of autumn foliage and trees to work from. Here, I added in the red tractor from my reference collection, as it helps draw the eye to the farm buildings.

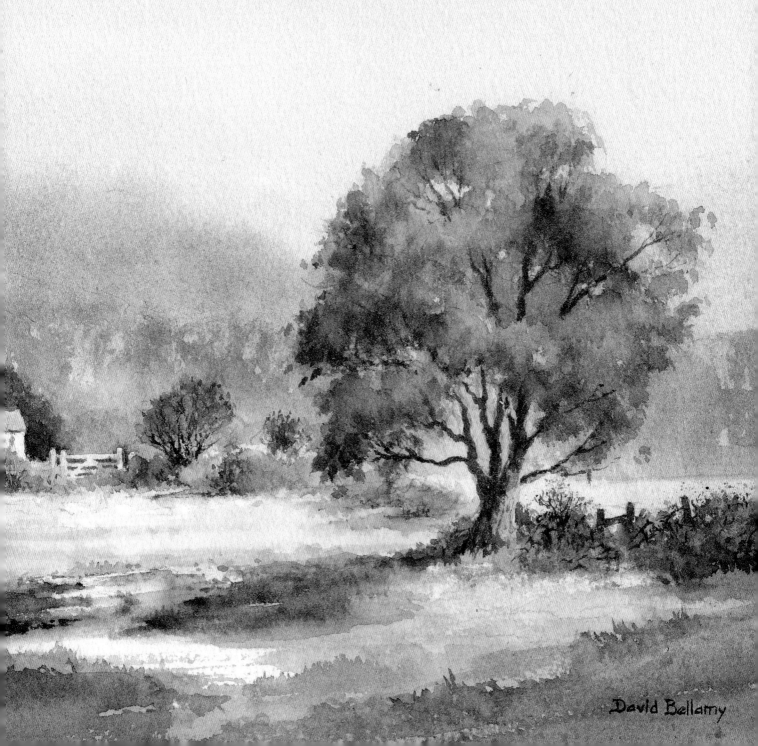

David Bellamy

Misty scenes

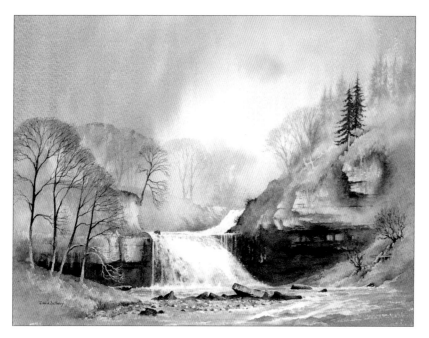

West Burton Force
28 x 35.5cm (11 x 14in), Rough

The wet-into-wet method, in which paint is added into a wash that is still wet, is normally the most effective way of suggesting a misty scene, but in this watercolour I have used two techniques as a way of suggesting varying degrees of mist. In the centre, directly above the more distant waterfall, a mixture of cadmium red with a touch of cobalt blue has been applied into a damp background wash of very weak yellow ochre to just faintly hint at the presence of trees in the mist. When the paper had dried completely, I used the same mixture with slightly more cobalt blue added to paint in the two trees that stand centrally above the main falls, while at the same time rendering the bank and rocks below them. I also added trees further to the left in the background. These features all dried slightly stronger than they now appear. Once the paper had dried, I gently sponged over the background trees with clean water and a natural sponge to push them back into the distance, though they are still strong enough to appear in front of those done wet into wet earlier. By combining these two techniques, you can create greater depth in misty scenes. The strongly etched tree on the left that looks as though it is about to fall into the pool adds further depth.

Glen Muick

20.3 x 30.5cm (8 x 12in), Not paper

Mist and fog can truly enhance the mood of a painting, but they are also effective devices where you wish to reduce the effect of a strident and dominating ridge, ugly background features, or repetitive detail such as the massed conifer slopes in this Highland scene. Here the wet-into-wet method really comes into its own, and if you wish to render the whole misty background in one go, you have to work quickly before the washes dry. Alternatively, you can work on one background section, allow that to dry completely, then re-wet the paper and move on to paint in the adjacent part of the background. If you are new to this technique, it is best to begin with simple compositions like the top left quadrant here, working up to more complicated effects when you gain confidence.

The autumn colours on the bushes are important to counter the overall drab grey-green, and it helps to position these where they will draw the eye to your centre of interest. Less prominent ones can be used to break up large areas of less importance and also create balance. Juxtaposing strong detail against misty passages will make your detailed features stand out. I have played down the detail in the water, as it is easy to overdo this, especially in turbulent rivers, but I splashed some yellow ochre into the falls. This suggests peat content and adds interest without the need for detail.

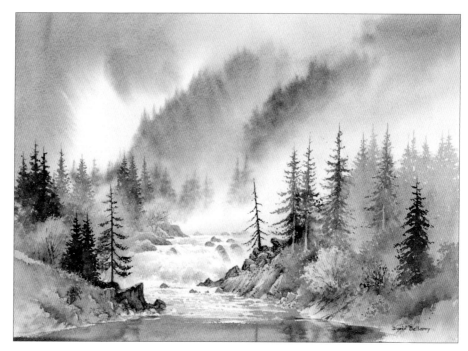

38

Colours for autumn scenes

There are endless combinations of mixtures for creating the colours of autumn, but I will just indicate a few of the more exciting examples here to give you a start. Experiment with a variety of colours to find what appeals to you most.

Quinacridone gold + cadmium red

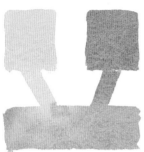

Quinacridone gold + transparent red oxide

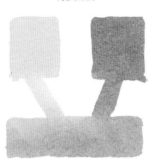

Gamboge + perylene violet

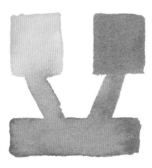

Quinacridone sienna + sodalite genuine

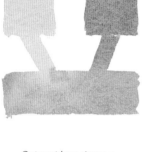

Lunar blue + transparent red oxide

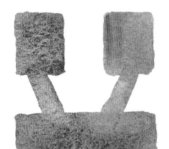

Aussie red gold + sodalite genuine

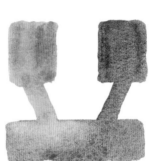

A selection of autumn colour mixtures

This is a selection of exciting colours you may like to try for your autumn paintings, but they are by no means the only ones. Although it is not an 'autumn colour,' I have included sodalite genuine to show how it not only darkens the colour with which it is mixed, but also introduces granulations, as shown here with Aussie red gold. Experiment with a wide variety of colours and keep swatches of them for future reference.

Autumn foliage with intermittent leaves

Light-coloured flecks of leaves and small clusters against a dark background can be really attractive, but they are annoyingly difficult to paint in watercolour. In this instance, I spotted masking fluid where I wanted light-coloured individual leaves – mainly at the edges of the foliage. You can also spatter with a toothbrush if you wish. On removing the mask, I dabbed in the bright yellows and reds, allowing them to run together in places. They stand out most clearly against the dark grey.

Emphasizing nature's warm colours

For these bushes I have used the powerful Daniel Smith colours Aussie red gold and transparent red oxide, then emphasized them by bringing in a background wash of French ultramarine and perylene violet, working round the single leaves quickly with a no. 8 round sable. As purple and gold are complementary colours, this creates a striking combination. Cadmium yellows and reds and gamboge also work well.

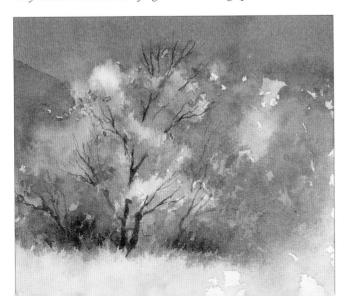

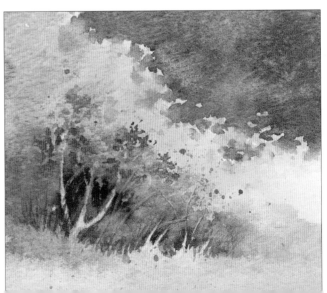

Observing and sketching autumn scenery

Critical observation and careful analysis of a scene are vital to create an authentic-looking result; try to develop these methods until they become second nature. Whether you are working from life or from a photograph, constantly compare the heights, sizes, tones, colour temperature etc. of each feature. Compare the brightness of adjacent colours and how they react with each other. Consider how you can emphasize the strength of colour or create strong contrasts to ensure a focal point stands out.

November colours

Sketching colours and their interaction is especially important with autumn colouring. As well as providing a record, sketching in colour shows you which colours work together. When you create a finished painting, you may wish to make changes so that one particular colour is juxtaposed against a different one to that in the sketch. Moving features slightly will achieve this.

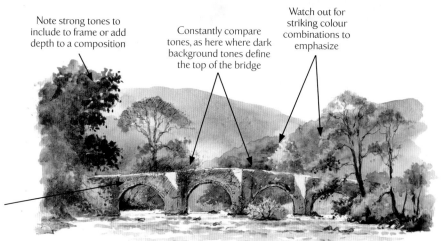

Note strong tones to include to frame or add depth to a composition

Constantly compare tones, as here where dark background tones define the top of the bridge

Watch out for striking colour combinations to emphasize

Study the interplay of light and shadow on various features

Capturing the flow of autumn colours

If the whole painting is covered in bright colours, it can be overwhelming. A patch of dullness can add impact to vibrant colours beside it. Splashes of brightness on or beside the focal point can really lift the work.

Observation and application

This painting was done from a winter sketch, with alterations to add vibrancy. I warmed up the foreground colours for autumn. The rough ground is a dried wash of Naples yellow with a darker, broken colour applied on top so that the yellow shows through. To add sparkle, I scratched with a scalpel across the centre to suggest a small pool of water. I exaggerated the cast shadow from the trees over the building to suggest a sunny autumn morning.

Brecon-Abergavenny Canal
25.4 x 33cm (10 x 13in), 425gsm (200lb) Not paper

I don't often throw the full gamut of autumn colours into a painting as it can become too overwhelming, but in this instance I decided to enjoy a more abandoned approach. Incidentally, this is an excellent idea if you feel that your painting is in a rut. This proved to be a popular painting. Note particularly how those autumn colours set against the pure white of the Saunders Waterford High White paper really stand out well.

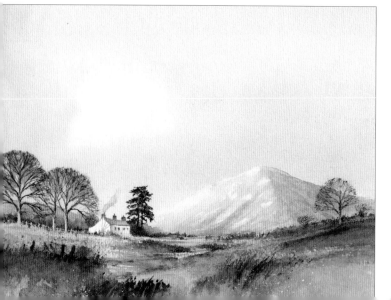

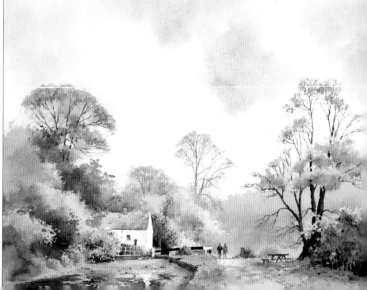

Autumn colours with a snowy background

The combination of autumn colours with early snow can create a striking composition, and I am always on the lookout for such possibilities. In this view above Little Langdale in the Lake District, there are warm autumn colours not just on the trees but also on the ground cover in places.

Track to Little Langdale

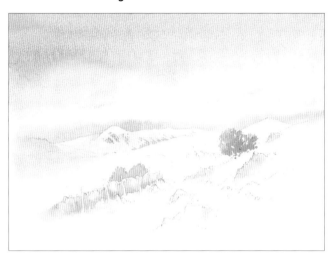

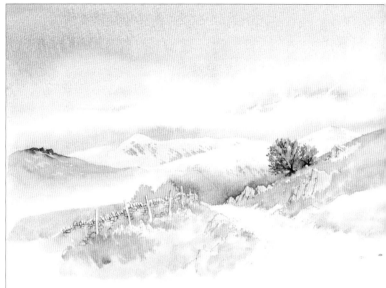

1 I painted the furthest mountain ridge in weak cobalt blue, blending it up into the sky so that the top edge was lost completely and the bottom made a sharp top edge for the white ridge below. The painting was then left to dry. Next, I began the sky at the top with a wash of lavender, a Daniel Smith colour with a gentle granulation. Lower down I introduced Naples yellow in the centre right, with touches of alizarin crimson, and in the lower part of the sky a weak wash of moonglow defined the two peaks and the long distant ridge. Moonglow was also used for rocky outcrops on the ridges. Next I rendered the wall with weak cobalt blue with a touch of cadmium red, and dropped in a little yellow ochre wet into wet. The trees were created with Aussie red gold with touches of transparent red oxide.

2 I softened some of the distant ridge edges with a damp flat brush, then painted in the dark crags on the left with moonglow. I also used this colour over the lower shadowy valley in the centre, fading it out at the top. Parts of the sky were strengthened to define the clouds. I delineated the trunks and branches on the right-hand trees with French ultramarine and burnt umber. Before finishing this stage I painted weak patches of green apatite genuine and transparent red oxide into the foreground area.

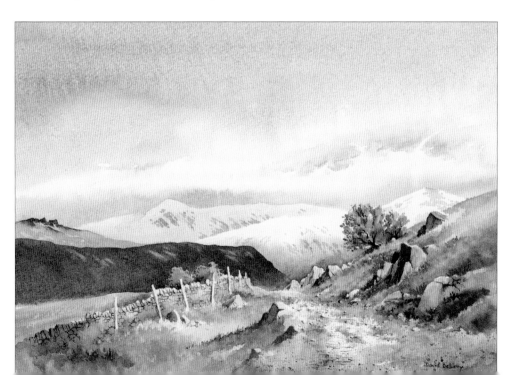

The finished painting
23 x 30.5cm (9 x 12in), 300gsm (140lb) Not paper

The dark middle ridge was rendered with strong moonglow, working round the small trees, and while it was still wet I pulled out a number of marks to suggest light crags and dropped in some transparent red oxide in places. Finally I tidied up the wall and rocks with detail using French ultramarine and burnt umber.

41

AUTUMN WATERFALL

As winter approaches, seek out woodland subjects, especially streams. A patch of sunlight on autumnal foliage can make the scene come alive. Combine it with a cascade or sparkling stretch of water and you have a subject worth painting. Backgrounds in woodlands are often best achieved using a misty wet-into-wet effect.

Materials used

Saunders Waterford 640gsm (300lb) Not watercolour paper

Brushes: Large and small squirrel mops, no. 7 and no. 4 sable round, 13mm (½in) flat, no. 3 rigger and 6mm (¼in) flat

Colours: Naples yellow, cobalt blue, cadmium red, alizarin crimson, yellow ochre, light red, quinacridone gold, cadmium yellow pale, burnt sienna, French ultramarine, cadmium orange, burnt umber

Masking fluid and old brush

Old toothbrush and paper mask

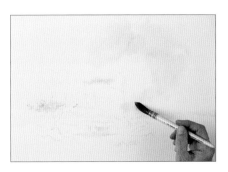

1 Draw the scene with a 3B pencil. Apply masking fluid to the lightest areas of foliage, the falling white water and a few splashes either side. Use a large squirrel mop to wash water over the background, down to the stream, then take the smaller squirrel mop and drop in Naples yellow over the foliage area.

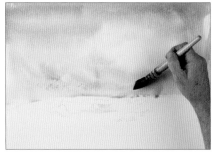

2 Brush a wash of cobalt blue and cadmium red across the sky, around the yellow, using the large mop, then brush in alizarin crimson and cobalt blue over the lower part of the sky.

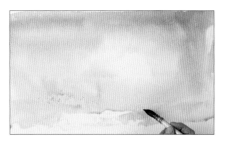

3 Use the smaller squirrel mop to paint yellow ochre across the ground so that it blends with the sky colour. Use a thirsty (barely damp) brush to pick up excess water. Soften the bottom with clean water to avoid a hard edge.

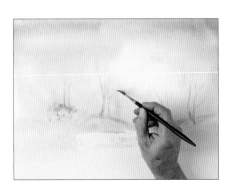

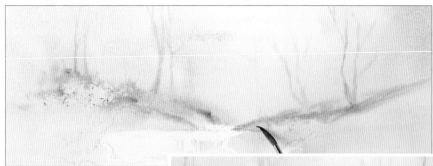

4 Use a no. 7 sable round with a good point and a mix of cobalt blue and light red to paint in the background trees wet into wet. Paint the edge of the ground and suggest bushes, putting darker tone round the masked foliage.

5 Add more light red to the mix to describe the contours of the ground nearer to the foreground. Working wet into wet, paint blobs of pure light red to suggest fallen leaves. Allow to dry. Change to a no. 4 sable round to blob quinacridone gold over the foreground. Allow to dry and soften any hard edges with a 13mm (½in) flat.

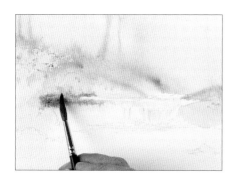

6 Use the no. 7 brush to paint a pale mix of cobalt blue above the white water. Add light red to darken the mix and sweep it across the water. Soften the edges with water.

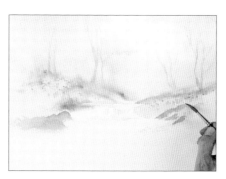

7 Pick up cadmium yellow pale with a little cobalt blue and a touch of cadmium red, and paint this onto the rocks to suggest moss. Soften the edges with clean water.

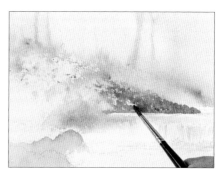

8 Mix cobalt blue with cadmium yellow pale plus a little burnt sienna and use the no. 4 brush on its side to paint the darker land behind the white water with dry-brush work. Add more burnt sienna to suggest dead leaves.

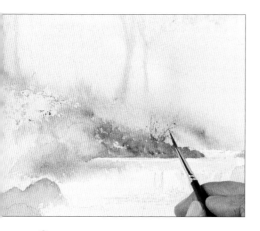

9 Use a no. 3 rigger to drag out paint from the wet wash, creating grasses and undergrowth.

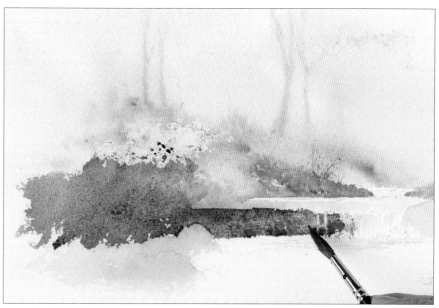

10 Mix French ultramarine and burnt sienna and use the no. 7 round to brush on the middle ground and the rock over which the white water runs. Drop in yellow ochre wet into wet.

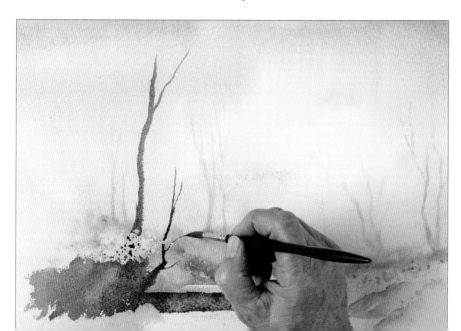

11 Use the same mix to paint tree trunks on the dry background. These sharper trees will push the previous ones into the background.

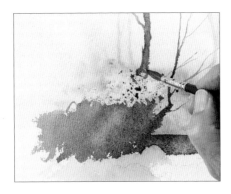

12 Add blobs of burnt sienna suggesting dried winter foliage, then drop cadmium orange into the wet tree trunk for texture and warmth.

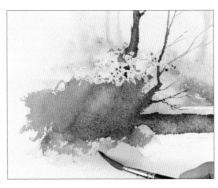

13 Mix burnt sienna with a little ultramarine and use the brush on its side to scrub the colour over the foreground moss.

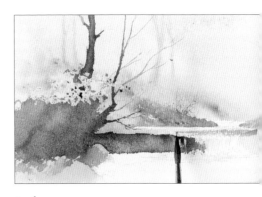

14 Paint cobalt blue with a touch of light red across the water to add tone, using the dry-brush technique.

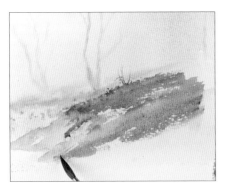

15 Use the same mix with a little more light red to sweep a broken wash across the land on the right, and add some vegetation with the point of the brush. Add tiny dots of burnt sienna for dried leaves.

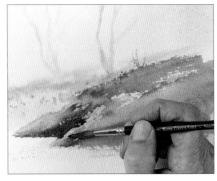

16 Make a darker mix of burnt sienna and cobalt blue and take this down to the water's edge, then soften it in with clean water.

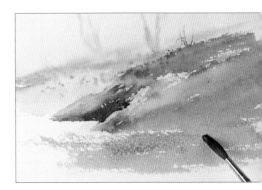

17 Carry the broken wash down to the foreground with the dry-brush technique, then drop in pure cobalt blue for variety.

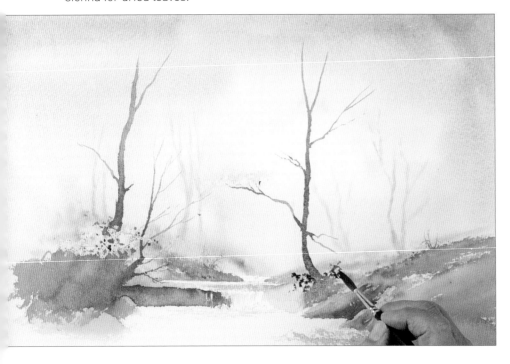

18 Paint the tree on the right with French ultramarine and burnt sienna, then drop in a green mix of cadmium yellow pale and cobalt blue lower down, wet into wet. Drop in yellow ochre higher up, then dot burnt sienna around the base of the tree for undergrowth and dead leaves.

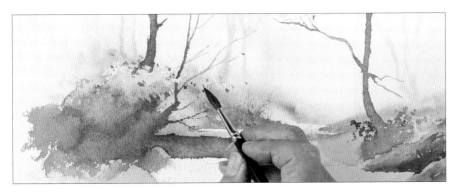

19 Remove the masking fluid from the foliage and use the 13mm (½in) flat to soften the resulting hard edges with water. Wash quinacridone gold across the foliage, then drop in cadmium yellow pale wet into wet. Drop in cadmium red. Add a few blobs of the same colour for winter leaves.

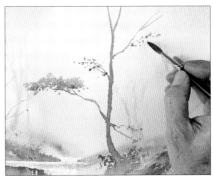

20 On the right-hand tree, the foliage is dark against light, so drop in light red first using the no. 7 brush, then quinacridone gold. Add foliage to the rest of the tree in the same way.

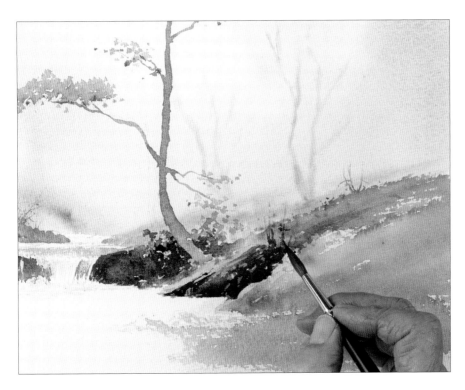

21 Make a dark mix of French ultramarine and burnt umber and paint the dark rocks near the water to define the bank. Drop in burnt sienna.

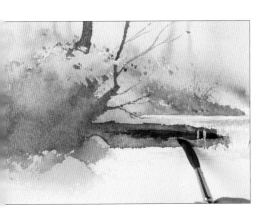

22 Mix burnt sienna and French ultramarine and paint the strata of the rocks to the left of the waterfall, then soften the edge with a damp brush.

23 Add texture to the right-hand tree trunk with the same mix and dry-brush work. Extend the branches and twigs.

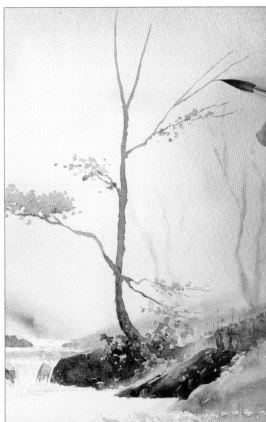

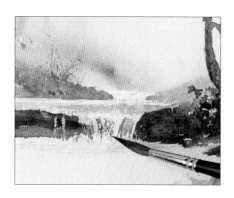

24 Use dry-brush work down the waterfall, over the masking fluid, with burnt umber and French ultramarine.

25 Add tone to the lower left-hand trunk with the same mix and drop in light red.

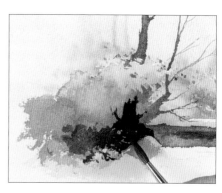

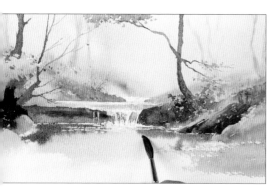

26 Wet the water area with clean water, then apply a pale mix of cobalt blue and cadmium red. Drop in a little Naples yellow, then paint wet-into-wet reflections with burnt umber and French ultramarine.

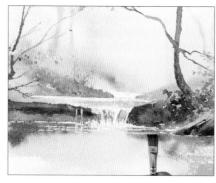

27 Use a damp 6mm (¼in) flat brush to lift out reflections of the white falling water, and ripples across the still water.

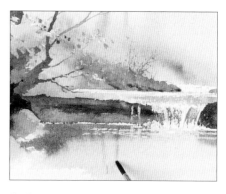

28 Use the no. 4 round brush and burnt sienna and French ultramarine to add a little detail to the far shore, then paint reflections of the background trees with cobalt blue and cadmium red.

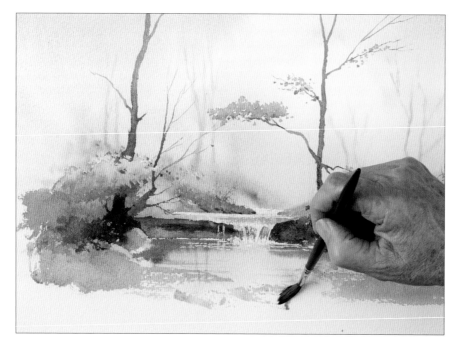

29 Add darks to the shadowed underside of the bright foliage on the left with cobalt blue and light red, then use the no. 7 brush to glaze this mix across the foreground. Pull it out to create texture on the water using dry-brush work. Allow to dry.

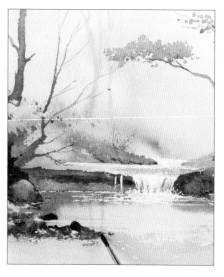

30 Remove the masking fluid from the waterfall and use the no. 4 brush and French ultramarine and burnt umber to add tone to it, then sharpen up the tone at the water's edge with the same mix, creating a rocky texture and adding more burnt umber as you come forwards.

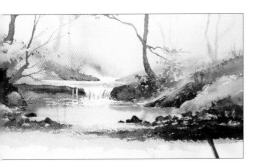

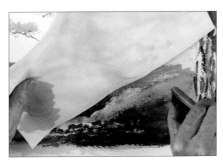

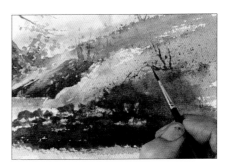

31 Drop yellow ochre into the left-hand rocks wet into wet. Create rocky texture on the right in the same way, then drop in light red.

32 Spatter the right-hand foreground with burnt sienna and a touch of cobalt blue using an old toothbrush and a paper mask.

33 Use the no. 3 rigger and burnt sienna and ultramarine to add twigs and other detail to the right-hand foreground. Stand back from the painting and make final adjustments such as strengthening tone or lengthening branches where required.

The finished painting.

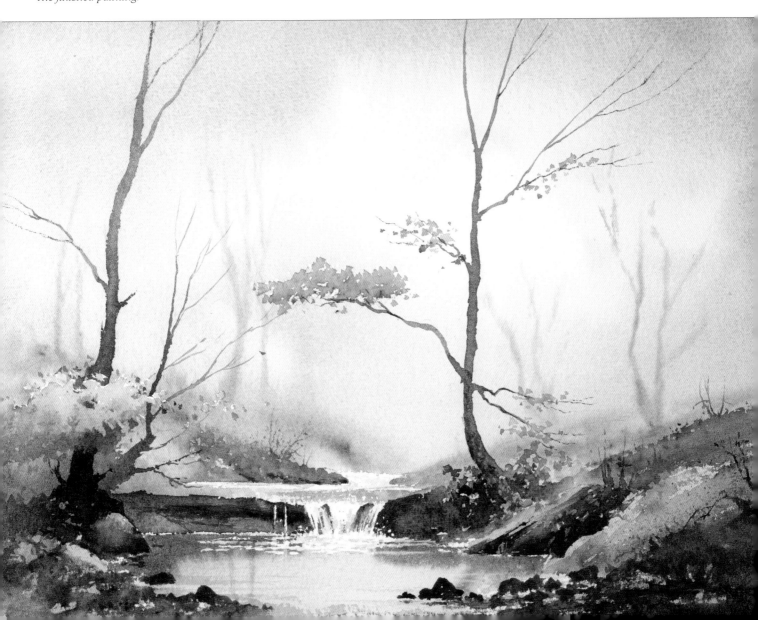

Winter

Winter to me is the most exciting of the seasons, and the most varied, with snow completely transforming the landscape. Gone are all those greens: we can see more of the features no longer hidden behind foliage, and although daylight hours are fewer, the low-angled sunshine creates evocative cast shadows to highlight features in a more dramatic way. Fields take on a greater range of colours and textures; tree trunks and branches display interesting and surprising colours. When seen as a mass, the branches of birch trees, for example, can take on a striking wine colour, especially useful if you wish to bring warmth into a cold snow scene. Dead leaves in trees and hedgerows and littered on the ground can be included even if they are not present, as their reds and oranges enliven the landscape and break up the masses of twigs and branches.

A fall of snow, even a light covering, brings a complete change to the countryside. Landscape features stand out more clearly against the whiteness. In watercolour we mainly use the white of the paper to suggest the whiteness of snow, but so much of the snow is most certainly not white because of shadow areas and colours in reflected light. Snow sometimes remains only briefly, so it is important to get out and record it as soon as possible. Note how it changes at different times of day. The onset of twilight can be a truly evocative time when warm-coloured skies create reflections in snowy fields, combined with long cast shadow.

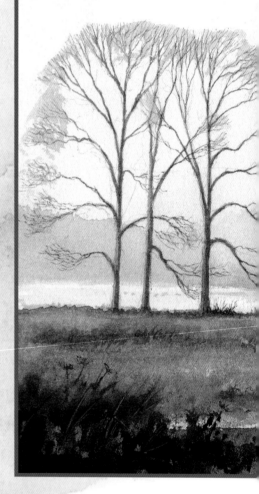

Wiltshire Barn
30.5 x 40.5cm (12 x 16in), 300gsm (140lb) Not paper

It can feel quite liberating painting a pastoral landscape without a preponderance of greens, and a versatile colour for winter fields is Naples yellow, slightly modified in places with the stronger yellow ochre or raw umber. Here I added raw umber after the wash of Naples yellow had dried, brushing it horizontally across the lower part of the field, dry-brush style. On the left-hand side, the Naples yellow stands out well against the background hills and trees, which were painted with French ultramarine and cadmium red.

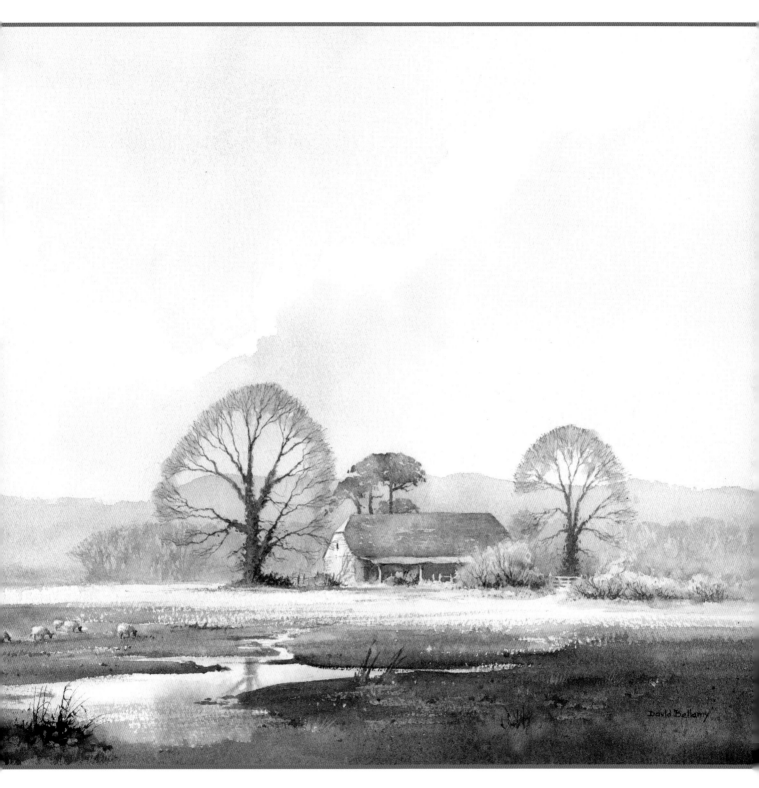

For the barn, I began with an overall wash of Naples yellow, and when this had dried, I laid light red across the roof, allowing the Naples yellow to show through in places. While the light red wash was wet, I added darker parts to the roof with a mixture of light red and French ultramarine, without much water on the brush. This approach created a more rustic, variegated roof. The side roof was painted with cobalt blue, and I created the details below it by painting in the dark negative shapes and adding a splash of cadmium red to draw the eye.

Though the sheep add life, I have kept them subdued in order to avoid conflicting with the barn as a centre of interest. I could have placed them closer to the barn, but then they would have been rather tiny. I included the puddle both to break up the foreground and to lead the eye towards the barn.

Working outdoors in winter

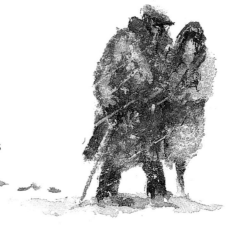

Your approach to sketching and painting outdoors in winter will be conditioned by your general experience of the outdoors. Some people enjoy being out in winter time and perhaps stopping to sketch for a limited period, while others loathe the idea.

I have always been an outdoorsman, and aware that without the right clothing, it can be purgatory hanging around outside in the cold. Layered clothing is better than thick garments. Modern thermal underwear that wicks away perspiration, covered with a warm shirt and a lined fleece jacket is an excellent combination, and over this a waterproof and windproof outer shell. A waterproof hood is of great help, but don't forget a woollen hat. Lined trousers are marvellous for outdoors in the cold. The thin but warm insulated gloves allow you to use a brush and pencil easily, although fingerless gloves, some with a flap to cover all while you are not sketching, are also available. If I am sitting around and not doing much walking, I often take a padded down jacket along, but it tends to get too hot if I walk any distance. All these items can be obtained in mountain gear shops and some fishermen's shops.

Not everyone can tolerate sketching outside, but there is still a lot you can do to obtain reasonable images. You need to prepare well. Keep your sketching equipment simple and ready for action. Have a flask of something hot ready to revive you. Don't forget to take photographs at various angles and zooming distances – a photograph may be enough for you to work from. Maybe you can work from the car: hatchbacks can make excellent places from which to sketch. Jenny, my wife, often uses hand-warmers in her gloves if it's really cold. A blanket in the car might also be sensible.

Wind blasting across snowy landscapes can be a real killer, so find some shelter if possible. At times, I have had to dart in and out of the shelter of a boulder or crag to render an important part of the scene that I can't quite see from my sanctuary, and moving around does help keep you warm. Many a time I have danced round rocks or trees to combat the cold, hoping that no one is watching! Walking and sketching is a superb way to work, as fifteen to twenty minutes of walking will generate plenty of heat to allow you to sketch for a while in all but the worst weather.

If you become concerned about the cold, then you need to get back into the warm as soon as possible. Often a few rapid strokes of the pencil may

The Pantiles, Tunbridge Wells

This pen and wash sketch was carried out over afternoon tea sitting outside a café in Kent, UK. Although winter was just about past, it was cold, but many like to sit outside even in the dead of winter, enjoying the sunshine, and so long as you are well wrapped up, carrying out a sketch while you take refreshments can be rewarding. Just don't dip your brush in the tea.

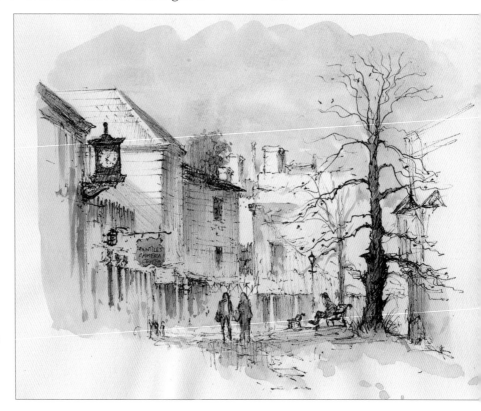

suffice to record the most important aspects of a scene. Then, once in a car, tent or building, note down any vital bits of visual information, such as colours, that you need to recall later. If there is a line of trees, all of the same species but different shapes and heights, I draw the most important one in a fair amount of detail and then simply create an outline to indicate the others. Later I can draw these in detail. I often start off the tone at a critical point in a passage and fill the rest in later. I am often amazed at how clearly I can recall elements, tones and even colours in a scene simply by looking at the mass of sketchy lines I have drawn with this visual shorthand method.

When sitting outside, it is easy to forget your situation when you are engrossed in an exciting composition, so you can become extremely cold without realising it. Remember to jump up every now and then and perhaps walk around vigorously for a minute or two.

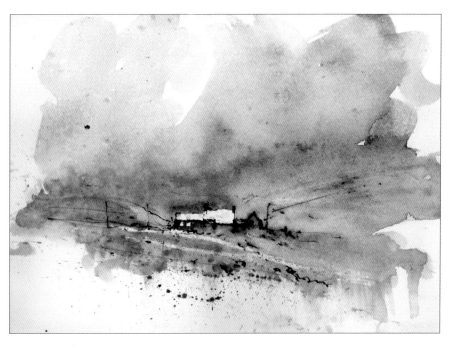

Farm at Shaw Bottom

Deep snow lay all around, but on the rough moor, much of it had been blown away or fallen into tall grasses and ditches. In this sketch, done on Hot Pressed paper, I rapidly splashed washes on with a no.10 round brush, avoiding the roofs, and immediately began drawing into the wet wash with a black watercolour pencil. I made the background darker in order to make the snow-covered roofs stand out starkly, and could see more of the horizon than is revealed in this sketch. While it was still damp, I pulled out some lighter areas with a flat brush and then spattered other colours over the foreground, some onto damp paper. Working quickly in this way gives a lovely sense of spontaneity, and there is less chance of frostbite for the artist.

Rapid watercolour sketching in the cold

For this I tend to lay washes down and then draw into them with a dark watercolour pencil as they are drying. This is fast and efficient and usually I can keep painting even when parts of the sketch remain wet, as a strong watercolour pencil line acts as a barrier, containing the wash, provided the angle of the paper is not too steep.

By sketching in this way, you learn to simplify a scene, seeking out the most important features and drawing and painting them with bold, confident strokes. This will immeasurably help your painting at home.

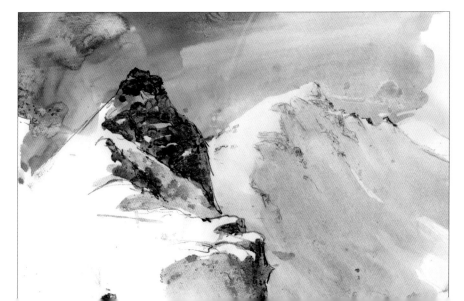

Summit of Parkhouse Hill

Sometimes the scene is simply too good to miss, whatever the weather conditions, and on this day they were frightful. I include this watercolour sketch because it shows that even with ferocious gusts and below-zero temperatures icing up the wash, you can achieve something that can be used as a basis for a later painting in the calm of the studio. Speed was achieved by using only one colour and drawing with a water-soluble pencil while the washes were still wet

Rogue colours in the landscape

There are normally far too many colours in the landscape in front of you, and we need to reduce these to impart a greater sense of unity to the scene. I rarely copy the colours before me, preferring to impose my own sense of colour, whether I feel the need for strongly contrasting colours or more harmonious ones. I always try to take into account the adjacent colours, as this has a strong bearing on how we see the whole effect.

One device I constantly use is to drop in what I call 'rogue' colours where I think the composition would benefit. These are often reds or yellows dropped into a wet patch of colour to warm it up. You will see examples of this approach throughout this book. It can be a strong red placed on a prominent tree trunk, a bright yellow field in front of a building, or a patch of Winsor blue amid some warmer blues in a snowy foreground.

Galway Coast
28 x 40.5cm (11 x 16in), 300gsm (140lb) Not paper

Although there tends to be more colour in the natural landscape in winter, it is often helpful to exaggerate the warm colours, both to draw the eye to a particular part of a composition, and to counter the coldness in a scene. In this painting of the Galway coast in Ireland, I have warmed up the strip of land below the cottage and the right-hand foreground with a rogue cadmium red, to alleviate the overall coldness of the scene and to give more prominence to the focal point.

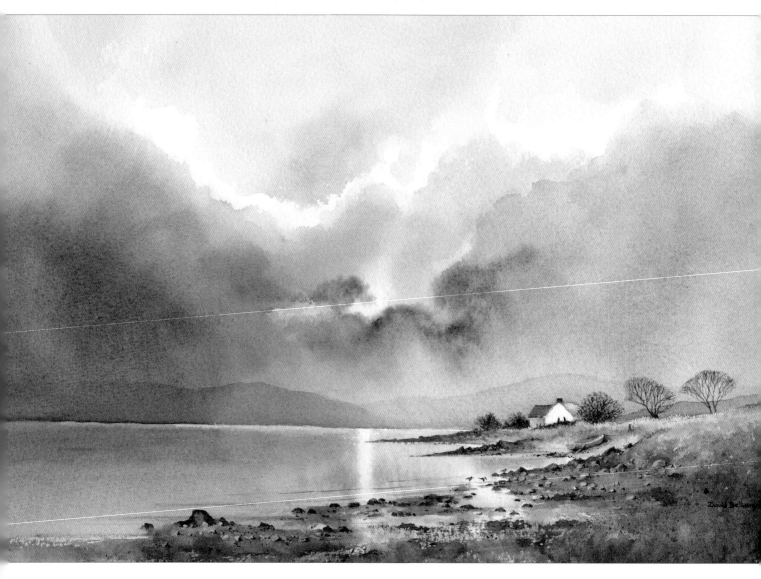

Taking advantage of low lighting

The lower angle of light during winter creates some wonderfully long and evocative cast shadows. This is especially apparent in early morning or evening, so you can create a lovely sense of evening by lengthening your shadows and combining this with warm light. Here we look at how I have suggested winter light in mid-morning.

Farm in Winter Sunlight
28 x 35.5cm (11 x 14in), 300gsm (140lb) Rough

Including cast shadows will really emphasize the feeling of sunlight, so take full advantage of long winter shadows, whether they sprawl over a building or field. In this painting the low winter light is coming from the left, throwing shadows from unseen trees across the foreground field. Note that all the fields and hillsides are either pale yellow or pale green – this affords maximum opportunity to make the cast shadows stand out. To accentuate this effect, I sometimes change a dull grey or ochre building into a whitewashed one. I used masking fluid to retain the light cut stalks leading towards the farm. Ruts, furrows and rows of stalks are an excellent way of leading the eye to the focal point.

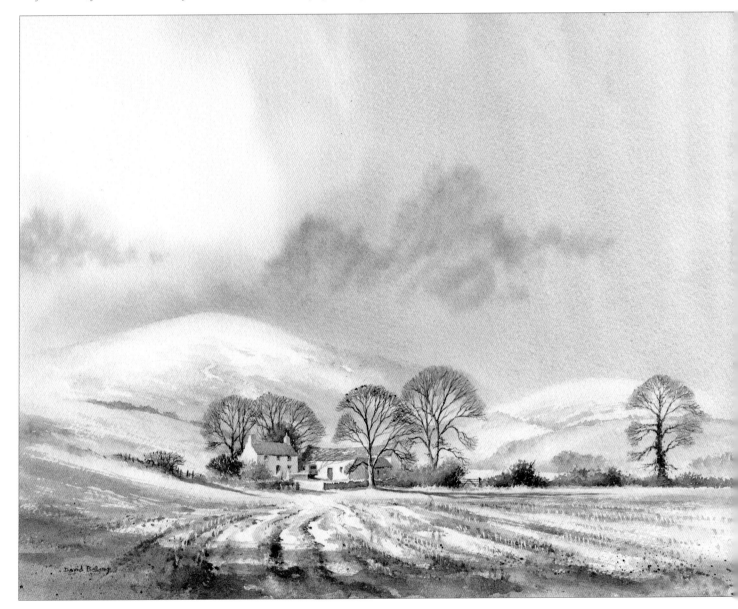

Bare branches and trunks

Winter trees and bushes have a charm and attraction that can enhance any landscape painting, and it is worth spending some time studying their characteristics. Tree trunks can be full of exciting and unexpected colours: reds, pinks, yellows, greens and blues, as well as the more common greys. The closer the tree stands, the more scope you have for including colour. Note, too, how branches hang, droop, curve or entwine themselves into amazing contortions. Here we look at a few examples.

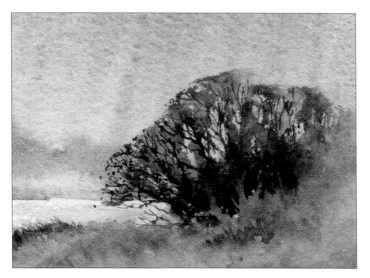

Negative tree trunks

An effective method with winter trees and bushes is to create a mass of branches and vegetation, apply negative painting into it to suggest trunks, then bring out the massed branchwork at the top. In this example, I started with a small wash of yellow ochre heightened with a touch of cadmium yellow pale, and immediately dropped in some weak Indian red above this, then a little burnt umber and French ultramarine above that, using the side of a no. 6 brush to suggest a mass of branches and letting all the washes intermingle. This gradual change of colour is a simple but effective technique. When the combined wash had dried, I described more branches with a rigger, over the upper burnt umber and French ultramarine wash. This gave a sense of depth to the branch structure. Finally I painted in the negative shapes between the trunks with a darker version of the French ultramarine and burnt umber mix.

Angular, sweeping or drooping branches

When you paint bare trees, note how the branches form as they leave the trunk: some shoot straight out, while others, such as thorn trees, are extremely angular. Others change direction dramatically or flow downwards in a graceful curve, like larch branches.

Choosing those special trees

Tree shapes make a fascinating study, and it is of great value to identify really good specimens and sketch and photograph them to keep as a reference for when you need that special tree. Sometimes the sub-branches leave the main branch in one direction only, as is mainly the case on the far left-hand trunk shown.

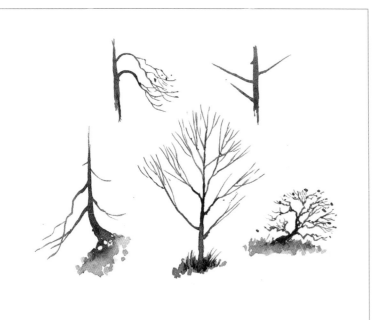

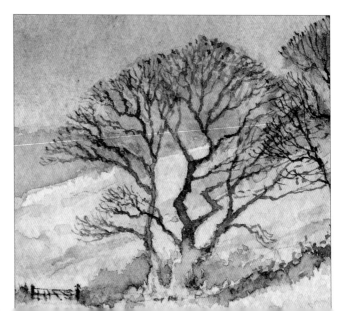

Painting light trees against dark skies and backgrounds

Light-coloured trees set against a dark, angry sky or sombre mountain can conjure up real drama, but they are not easy to paint in watercolour. You may be able to see every single branch strongly etched against the darkness, but try to avoid any attempt at putting them all in. Negative painting techniques are almost impossible to render convincingly if you try to emulate a great mass of branches. In these examples I show how masking fluid can work well for this effect.

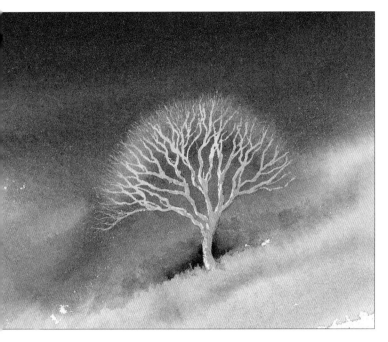

Light tree against a dark sky

In this example I have resorted to masking fluid for the main branches, applied with a size 0 rigger with most of the masking fluid removed from the brush, so that a fine line was achieved for the outer branches. You have to waste some masking fluid on scrap paper first to check that it is fine enough for your needs. After the dark sky was painted over the light trees, I removed the masking fluid, then scrubbed the top mass of branches with a small, damp, flat brush. This suggests the mass of light twigs and branches. It also leaves a pleasing fuzzy edge to the extremities. I laid a weak glaze of French ultramarine and cadmium red over the right-hand (shadow) side of the tree, and this also helped to prevent it looking like a cut-out.

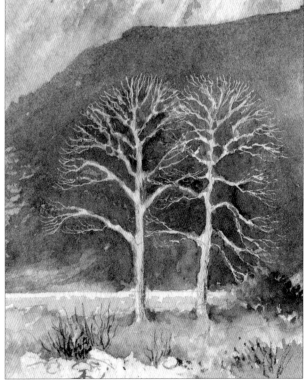

Light trees against a mountainside

In this example, I again used masking fluid for the trunks and main branches, but this time I painted the mass of twigs and smaller branches with white gouache, using a size 0 rigger.

Winter Mountains

In winter, places like Buttermere in the Lake District, UK, are easier to access than in summer, when they can be choked with people and traffic. You don't have to walk far to get a decent viewpoint, and can always retire to the pub if the weather gets too much. In winter, the mountainsides can reveal many warm colours, which you can move to suit your composition. A cool-temperature passage or two works wonders for balance and will make your warm areas appear even warmer.

Materials used

Saunders Waterford 640gsm (300lb) Rough watercolour paper

Brushes: Large and small squirrel mops, no. 7 and no. 4 sable round, 13mm (½in) flat, no. 10 sable round, no. 1 rigger

Colours: Naples yellow, yellow ochre, cadmium orange, cobalt blue, French ultramarine, burnt umber, cadmium red, Indian red, light red, quinacridone gold, green gold, raw umber, alizarin crimson

Sponge; paper mask; 6B pencil

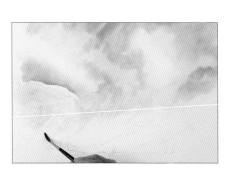

1 Draw the scene with a 6B pencil. Wash the sky and mountains with a large squirrel mop and clean water, then wash Naples yellow and a little yellow ochre over the area, followed by Naples yellow and cadmium orange on the right. Mix a little of the orange with cobalt blue and wash this diagonally across for cloud.

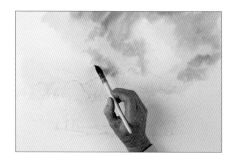

2 Working wet into wet, paint in darker cloud with French ultramarine and burnt umber, leaving hints of white and suggesting cloud boiling up over the mountains. Allow to dry.

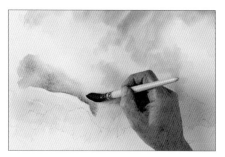

3 Paint the background ridge with pale cobalt blue and yellow ochre, on a fairly dry no. 7 round brush. Use the small mop to rewet the sky behind this and darken it with burnt umber and French ultramarine to highlight the ridge.

4 Use the no. 7 round and dry-brush work with cobalt blue and yellow ochre to paint the scree on the mountain slopes.

5 Paint the rocky area in the middle ground and foreground with yellow ochre, then paint Naples yellow for the trees on the right, which will be light against a dark background.

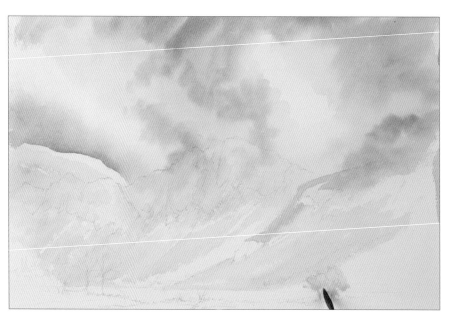

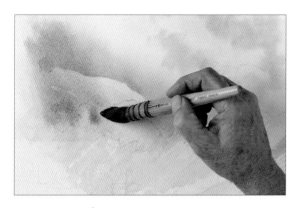

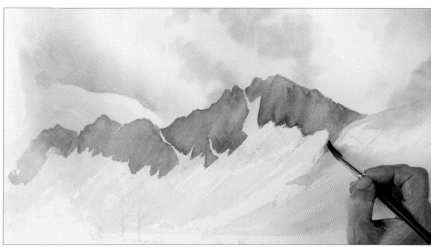

6 Use a damp 13mm (½in) flat brush to soften the hard edge of the background ridge, then use a large mop brush to paint water over the left-hand side of the painting and apply a glaze of cobalt blue and cadmium red. Allow to dry.

7 Mix light red and ultramarine and use the no. 10 round brush to paint the crags of the mountains wet on dry, then drop in yellow ochre. Continue across the painting in this way.

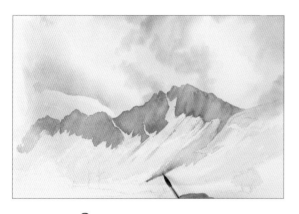

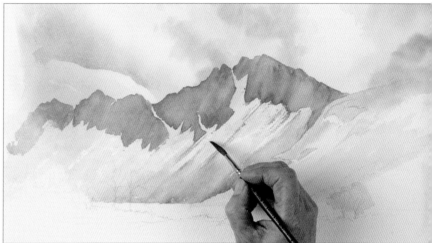

8 Use a paler version of the same mix with a no. 7 brush to paint behind the foreground ridge on the right. Drop in Indian red wet into wet.

9 Rewet the middle area and drop in light red, then Indian red at the bottom. Allow to dry.

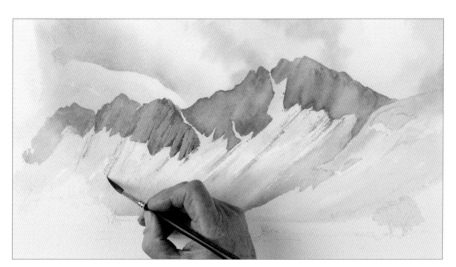

10 Suggest detail on the crags and the lower slopes with the same mix and dry-brush work.

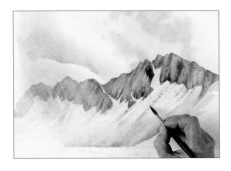

11 Wipe a damp sponge diagonally over the left-hand side of the mountains to subdue them, then use the point of the no. 7 brush to paint detail of the middle crags with French ultramarine and burnt umber.

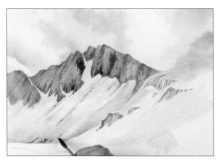

12 Paint more rocky detail on the right-hand side in the same way, and continue on the lower slopes.

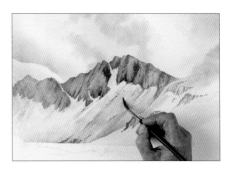

13 Add yellow ochre to the slopes.

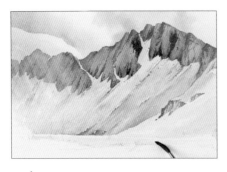

14 Drag a pale mix of cobalt blue across the lake, leaving speckles of white, and allow to dry. This brings out the warmth of the colours behind it.

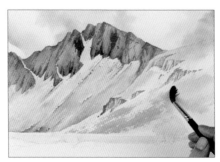

15 Use the no. 10 brush on its side to paint broken colour across the right-hand slope with light red, then soften the edges with water. Add more yellow ochre.

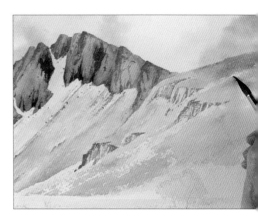

16 Paint quinacridone gold on the surfaces catching the light to highlight them. Blend in a mix of French ultramarine and light red.

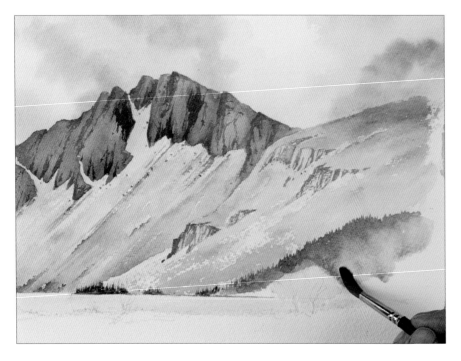

17 Use the no. 7 round and a mix of ultramarine and raw umber to paint conifers on the far shore. Continue them along the lakeside to the right, changing to green gold and cobalt blue. Soften the bottom of the shape with water.

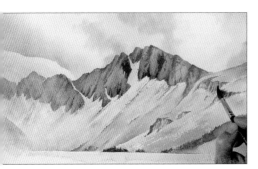

18 Paint a very pale slope of French ultramarine and light red on the far left, then add shadow to the right-hand crags with cadmium red and cobalt blue. Allow to dry.

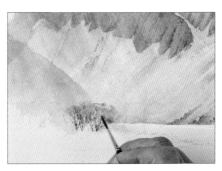

19 Use the no. 4 round brush and raw umber to paint the area of trees on the left, then use the no. 1 rigger and a mix of burnt umber and French ultramarine to paint trunks and branches.

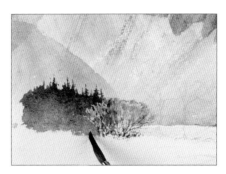

20 Paint conifers to the left using the point of the no. 7 brush and a mix of raw umber and French ultramarine. Paint round the lighter trees. Drop in quinacridone gold.

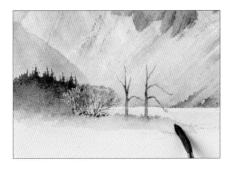

21 Use the same mix and brush to paint the two main trees on the left, then drop in green gold while the trunks are wet. Paint green gold beneath the trees as well.

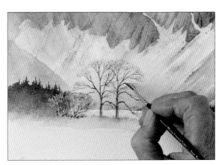

22 Change to the no. 1 rigger and paint the finer branches with burnt umber and French ultramarine.

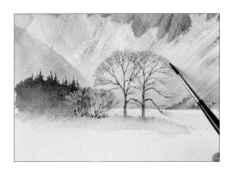

23 Use a weaker mix of the same colours and the no. 4 brush on its side to create the twigwork.

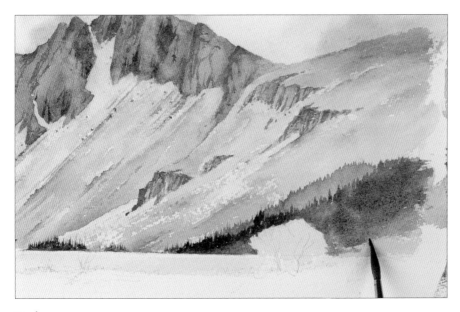

24 Use the no. 7 brush and a green mix of French ultramarine and raw umber to paint the darker conifers on the right-hand lakeside. Paint the pointed tops first, then scrub in the broader area.

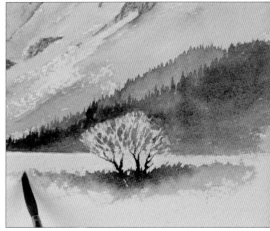

25 Suggest the light winter trees against the dark background with negative painting, then paint the trunks and details with French ultramarine and burnt umber. Drop in light red at the base of the trees, then yellow ochre wet into wet.

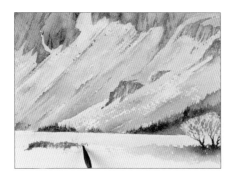

26 Paint the dry-stone wall in the foreground with French ultramarine and raw umber.

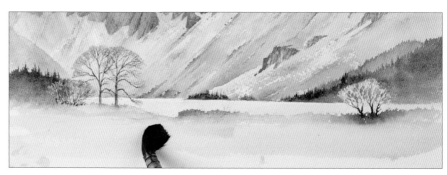

27 Use the small squirrel mop to sweep in a wash of yellow ochre in the foreground. Allow to dry.

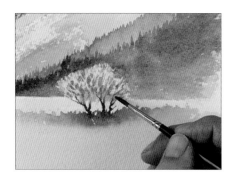

28 Use the no. 4 brush with a pale mix of French ultramarine and a hint of burnt umber to suggest shadow in the lighter trees.

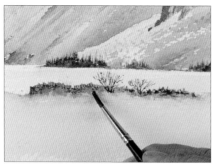

29 Change to the no. 1 rigger and a mix of burnt umber and French ultramarine and suggest bushes against the wall. Hint at stones, especially capstones. Add tone in the wall to subdue the stonework.

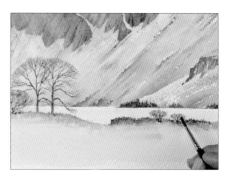

30 Darken under the left-hand trees with a little raw umber, then apply alizarin crimson to the bushes for twigwork.

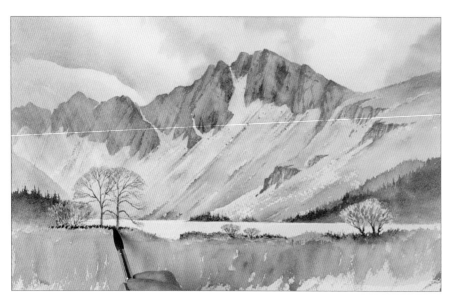

31 Darken the foreground with the no. 10 brush on its side and a mix of cobalt blue and yellow ochre, creating texture. Drop in cadmium red to liven it up, and light red at the edge of the lake. Darken under the trees with French ultramarine and burnt umber.

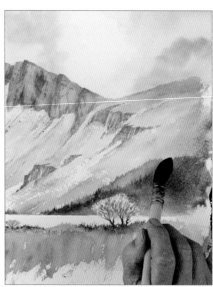

32 Subdue the right-hand conifers with the small mop brush, first with clean water, then a glaze of cobalt blue and cadmium red.

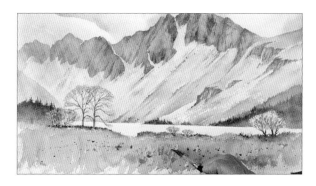

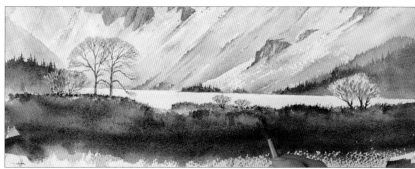

33 Spatter light red and French ultramarine in the foreground from a paintbrush, then drop in more light red and use the no. 7 brush to flick up grasses.

34 At this point I stood back from the painting and decided to darken the foreground. Load the large mop brush with burnt umber and French ultramarine and sweep it over the foreground. Dot suggested detail over the glaze to reinstate it and drop in Naples yellow and light red. Spatter some water across the damp wash to add texture.

The finished painting.

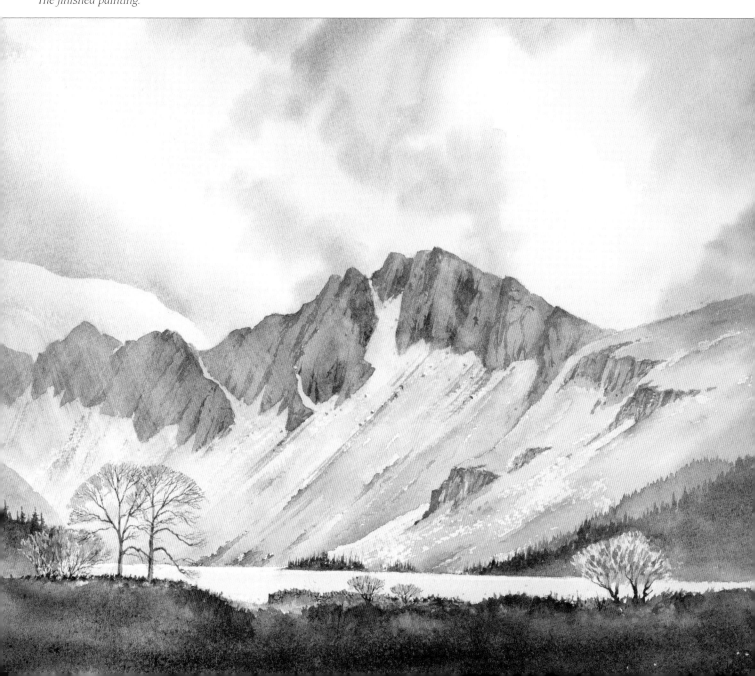

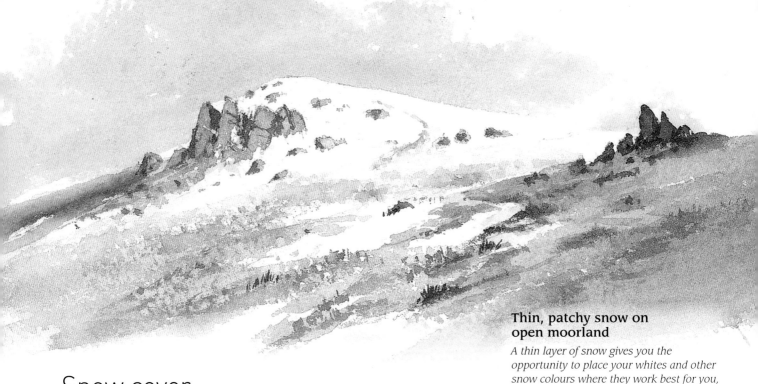

Snow cover

Snow cover can vary considerably from thin, patchy effects to deep snow obliterating almost everything, and the transition from snow-covered hills to the bare ground can cause painters problems. By studying these varied effects, you will be in a better position to alter a scene to your advantage, so when you encounter the next fall of snow, consider how you can render these effects to make the most of the changed landscape.

Transition from snow

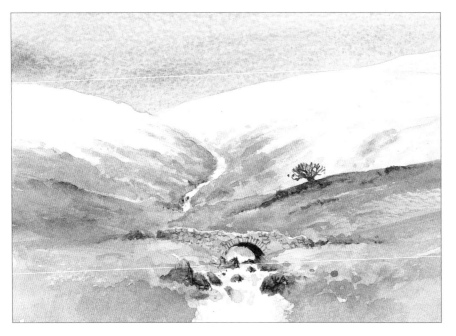

Thin, patchy snow on open moorland

A thin layer of snow gives you the opportunity to place your whites and other snow colours where they work best for you, as well as laying in the warmer colours of the bare ground to best advantage. Don't have too many fiddly little patches of snow, though, as it will look messy. In this example, you will see both hard and soft transitions between snow and untouched ground, and note the winding path which is white in the foreground where snow has accumulated, and dark as it crests the upper slope in the snow. The light red has been applied with a dry brush, blending in some of the edges with a damp brush. It's amazing what magic you can find in such a simple scene, just by spending a few minutes observing the land.

Bridge scene

Painting a snow-covered background of hills and mountains, while retaining a snow-free foreground, can be an attractive way of working. It does not have to be all snow, and sometimes when snow has melted, foregrounds can appear really messy. The transition from snowy areas can be achieved in different ways. On the right, you will see how a dark ridge, painted with light red and burnt umber, stands out hard against the snowy background, while on the left, the transition is more gradual. For this latter effect, you can wet the paper first and then take the ground colour up into the wet area – yellow ochre in this case, tinged in places with a mid-grey made up of cobalt blue and light red. An alternative method is to paint on to dry paper with the side of your brush, or simply to brush upwards with a dry brush, as in the craggy moorland sketch above.

Using a candle resist

Another technique for representing intermittent snow cover is to drag a candle across the required part of the painting, as in this Dartmoor scene. The wax will resist watercolour washes.

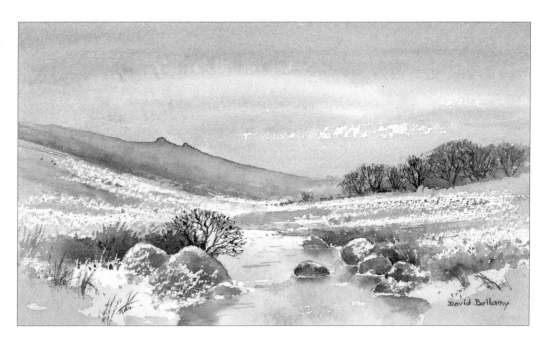

Vibrant colours in the snow – Herefordshire Lane

15.2 x 20.3cm (6 x 8in), 640gsm (300lb) Not paper

Foregrounds are rarely easy, and often snowy ones can appear almost devoid of any detail, so that we may be tempted to paint in all manner of vegetation sticking out of the blank whiteness. One method I enjoy is splashing in a number of colours – usually different blues, but sometimes even a red, despite it being quite the opposite to anything present in the scene. In this small watercolour, I have added some Winsor blue and permanent rose to join the wash of French ultramarine and cadmium red. The white trees were achieved with masking fluid, with some of the branches washed over after the mask was removed, to create more shadowy branches.

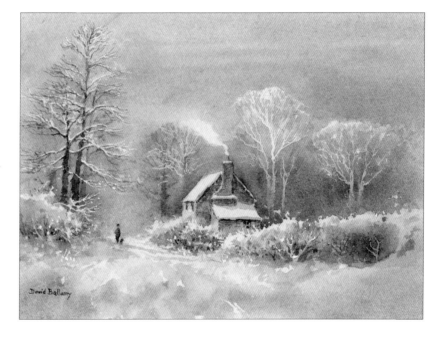

Moorland Farm

In this composition, you can see various tones on the snow-covered fields, and in particular the change of tone where the hills meet the sky: the hill is simply white paper against a dark sky on the left, and blue-grey against a lighter sky on the right. Planning this out before you start painting will reap excellent rewards. Note how the hedgerows are not continuous. Rather than paint in detailed vegetation sticking out of the foreground snow, I have simply splashed in patches of yellow ochre in a few places, a useful alternative to over-detailing this rather vulnerable part of a painting.

63

Landscape under deep snow

This scene in North Staffordshire, UK, immediately appealed: deep snow simplified the composition, the road formed an excellent lead-in to the centre of interest, and strong afternoon sunlight created interesting cast shadows and highlights.

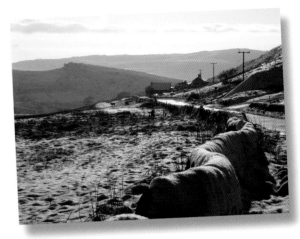

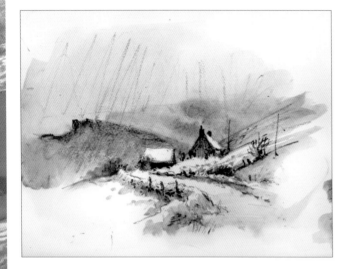

The actual scene was almost a monochrome and could well have been painted as such. At times, winter presents us with a monochrome, so take advantage of these interesting situations, which can exude a powerful sense of mood.

Colour sketch

With an indigo water-soluble ink block, I drew in the main features, then applied tone in varying strengths, before washing over the sketch with a wet brush. This is a quick way of producing a sketch and the water-soluble ink block encourages you to avoid describing too much detail.

Farm at Flash Bottom
25.4 x 15.2cm (10 x 6in), Rough

The lower sky and distant hills were painted with washes of French ultramarine and cadmium red, with the far ridge appearing and disappearing in places. The white parts were left as untouched paper. I added a red muck spreader beside the farmhouse for interest and colour, and the cast shadows gave a strong feeling of sunlight. Blobs of phthalo blue in the foreground create additional variation.

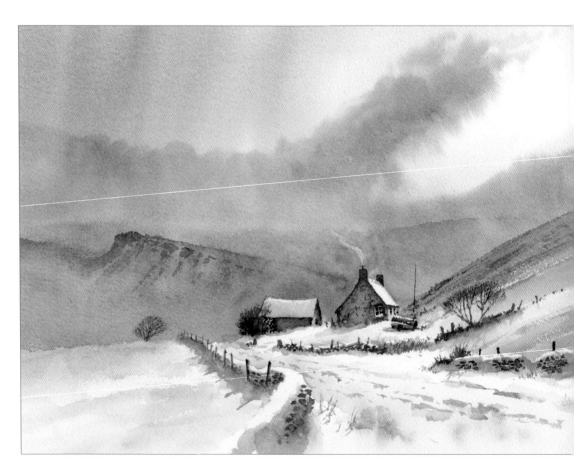

Introducing colour to snow scenes

Unless you are intent on portraying a thoroughly cold environment, totally devoid of any hint of warmth, it makes for a more attractive composition if you introduce an element of warm colour into a snow scene. This can be achieved by painting the sky in warm colours, creating warm-coloured reflections in water, ice or snow, or introducing warm-coloured vegetation, figures or objects. Even a small splash of bright colour can make a difference.

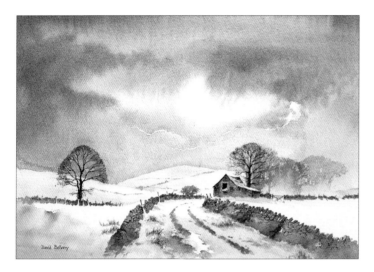

Yorkshire Barn
20.3 x 28cm (8 x 11in)

Snow scenes can appear really cold and uninviting if there is a lack of warm colour. In this landscape, the warm colours in the sky, barn, dry-stone walls and smattering of vegetation all add up to a more welcoming snow scene. I deliberately took some time to work out the sort of sky I wanted, and where to place the warm colours. A studio sketch carried out in colour will help you work this out.

Massed trees and snow

A subtle way of increasing the warmer feeling of your snow scenes is by mixing or dropping in warmer colours instead of perhaps more neutral ones. In this landscape, I have dropped light red into the lower half of the massed trees to give it a lovely warm sensation, instead of using a colour like burnt umber to create a cooler, greyer overall effect.

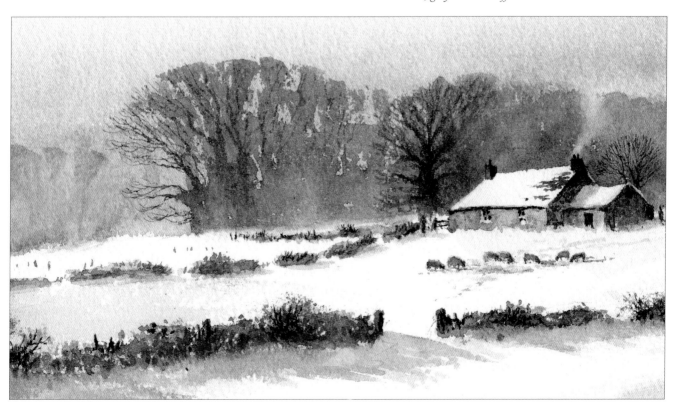

Depicting snow and ice on trees

Ice patterns and snow on trees can range from the ordinary to the spectacular, and they can be further enhanced by the surrounding atmosphere and light. Sometimes the effect of ice-rimed branches can be so overwhelming that any attempt to render such intricate, icy detail will look overworked. Aim for brief glimpses of stunning detail in a lost-and-found manner, and use colour and tone as a substitute for detail in places.

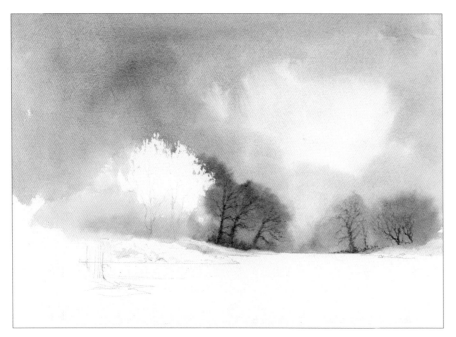

At this first stage, masking fluid was applied to the top branches of the birch trees. I then laid a fluid wash of Naples yellow on the right-hand part of the sky, then a mixture of French ultramarine and cadmium red over most of the sky. A stronger mix of the same colours, applied wet into wet, suggested the more distant tree mass, then a very strong mixture was applied with a fine rigger to draw in the main trunks. When the paper had completely dried, the masking fluid was removed.

Snow, Ice and Mist on the Wye
23 x 30.5cm (9 x 12in), 300gsm (140lb)
Not paper

I painted more Naples yellow onto the main trees to suggest a slight warming of colour temperature, then the shadow areas with French ultramarine and cadmium red. Yellow ochre was laid over the reeds and vegetation. For the river, after wetting the whole area with clean water, I painted weak Naples yellow in the centre, suggesting some colour reflection from the sky. I then added French ultramarine and burnt umber, running it into the Naples yellow. A light patch of ice was created on the left by working negatively round the shape.

Once everything was dry, I re-wetted the river on the left and applied a strong wash of ultramarine and cadmium red into the darkest reflections, thus highlighting the reflections of the lighter snow-covered bank. Finally I scratched out slivers of light with a scalpel.

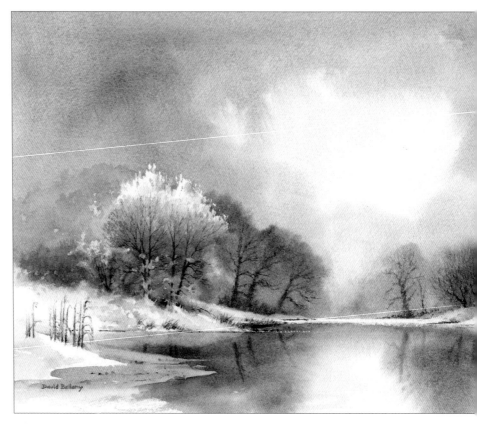

Animals in cold conditions

There is something very appealing and heart-tugging about animals caught in cold snowscapes. Like humans, they often hold themselves in such a way as to show they are suffering from the cold.

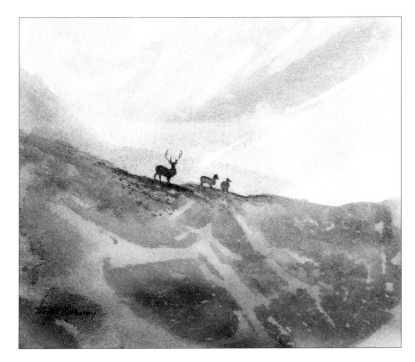

Highland Deer
15.2 x 20.3cm (6 x 8in), 300gsm (140lb) Rough

Most artists enjoy trying new techniques. Occasionally, when the subject seems right, I use plastic food wrap to create interesting patterns. This works especially well with snow and ice scenes. Here I applied fluid washes of Winsor blue, at the same time leaving patches of untouched paper to suggest the snow highlights. While this lay wet on the paper, I placed a sheet of plastic food wrap over it and dragged it slightly to the left to suggest a sense of direction. I then left the food wrap in place and allowed the wash to dry. After the paper had completely dried, I removed the food wrap and then painted in the rest of the scene as normal. Sometimes I refrain from doing any pencil drawing until after the washes have dried, thus allowing me to take advantage of how the plastic food wrap has affected the paper.

Cattle Feeding
17.8 x 25.4cm (7 x 10in), 300gsm (140lb) Not paper

Animals make excellent centres of interest, their appeal accentuated when set in a bleak landscape. Note in this work how background features have been deliberately managed to make the animals stand out. The black Friesians to the rear are silhouetted against a purple-grey hedgerow, totally lacking in detail, while the right-hand beast has a light-coloured back that is clearly etched against the dark bush.

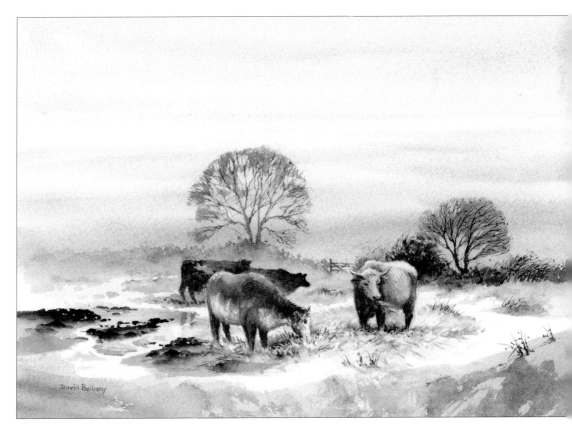

Capturing a castle in watercolour

On this occasion the atmosphere was constantly changing and the washes slow to dry, so outdoor watercolour sketching was challenging, with the great temptation to change my response as conditions altered. That can be fatal to a work, so either do a second sketch or take several photographs as things change.

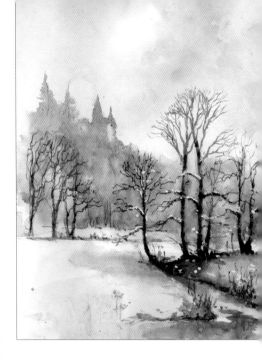

This viewpoint appealed to me, as the building rose above the trees, all in sunlight apart from the foreground. For this watercolour sketch, I drew into the wet washes with a black watercolour pencil to speed things up. Even so, the sketch took a long time in slow drying conditions, and by the time I had completed it, the sun had disappeared and ground mist created a magical, ethereal atmosphere. In the resulting painting, I decided to incorporate both the sun on the castle and higher trees, and the mist lower down.

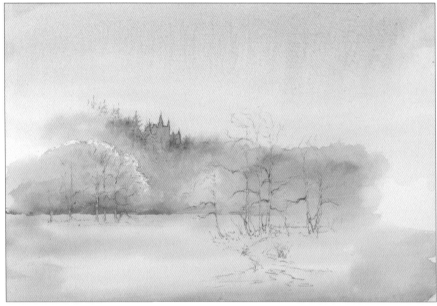

1 I began by laying a wash of cobalt blue over the upper sky, and yellow ochre over the lower part, bringing it down over the trees near the castle. While this was wet, I touched in some weak light red, then allowed it to dry. I painted on masking fluid with an old size 0 rigger for the snow-clad branches, then laid Winsor blue over the lower part of the composition to create a cool effect, though adding in some light red over the left-hand tree mass.

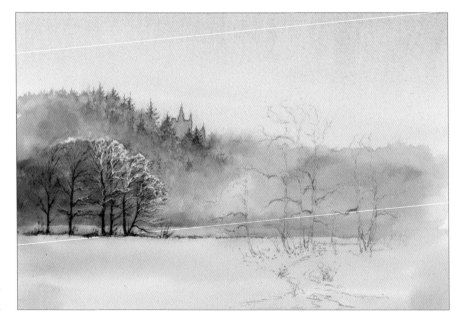

2 I concentrated on the left-hand trees by drawing in the trunks and branches with a mixture of Winsor blue and light red. When this had dried, I removed the masking fluid just from this area, then laid a weak glaze of Winsor blue across the lower section of the left-hand trees.

Alton Castle, Staffordshire

20.3 x 28cm (8 x 11in) 300gsm (140lb) Not paper

With the paper completely dry, I sponged horizontally across the lower part of the left-hand trees to suggest mist, using a soft natural sponge and clean water and dabbing off the excess liquid afterwards. This combination of glazes and sponging is effective for suggesting mist. I then created a shadow band horizontally across the picture, below the band created for the mist, with a weak mixture of Winsor blue and light red. The right-hand tree trunks were rendered with a stronger combination of Winsor blue and burnt umber, followed by a weaker mix of the same colours over the right-hand foreground. To suggest the varied tones in the icy water, I used the same mixture in various degrees of strength. Finally I put in the foreground shadows and vegetation.

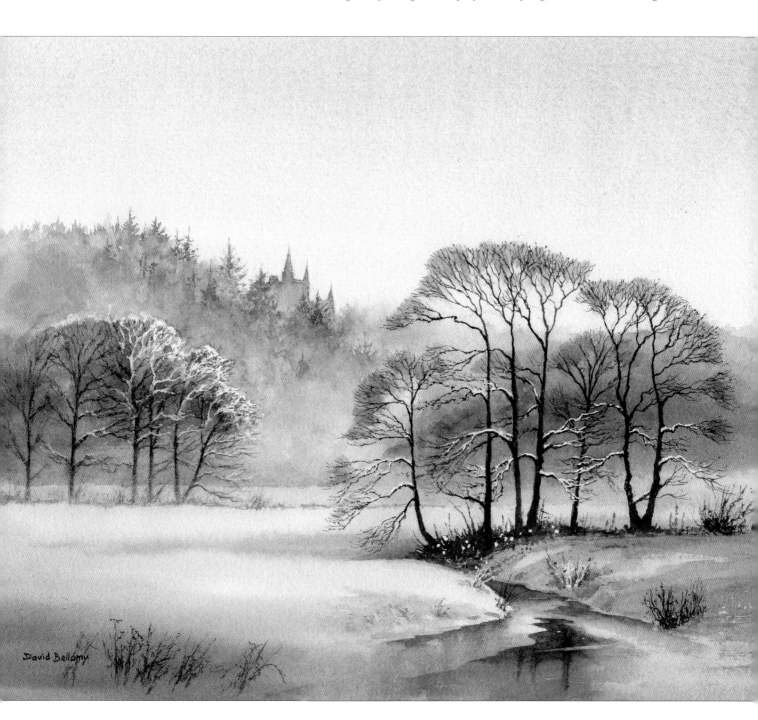

David Bellamy

Falling snow

Gently falling snow can be attractive, and is fairly easy to accomplish. Blizzards on the other hand are not so easy. Blizzard effects can vary from the hard-driven type to those where occasional, gentler eddies and flurries of snow stand against a background of indefinite images. It is fascinating to experiment with these effects.

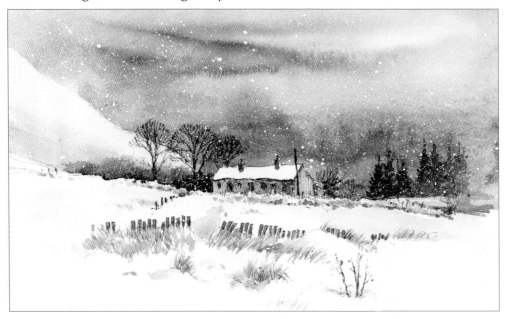

Gently falling snow

The falling snow was created by spattering white gouache with a toothbrush – simply load the toothbrush with gouache and then drag your thumb or a palette knife across it. Test it out first on scrap paper with a dark image, as too much water on the brush can result in huge ugly blobs. You may find it helpful to darken certain passages of the composition to a degree so that the white gouache stands out.

Blizzard in Glen Feshie, Scottish Highlands

20.3 x 25.4cm (8 x 10in), 640gsm (300lb) Rough

I began with a wash of water over the sky, then applied Naples yellow above where the trees would appear. To this I added a weak wash of cadmium orange to warm the sky slightly. A strong mixture of burnt umber and indigo was then laid across most of the sky apart from the area left light, making the right-hand side slightly darker. I waited for a few moments before suggesting some of the pine trees, in two stages to give depth. I waited a further few minutes until the degree of dryness seemed right, then applied the stronger, slightly warmer mixture of burnt umber and indigo to define the main mass of pines.

When the right-hand side of the sky was at the right stage of drying, I used a damp 13mm (½in) flat brush without any colour, with short, energetic diagonal strokes, to suggest the violent movement of the blizzard across the sky and pines. I then picked up some white gouache to strike across the damp paper. Note that you need to use a 'thin' flat brush for this. When the paper was dry, I spattered it with white gouache on a toothbrush, at a low angle, first using a wettish application for the fainter, falling snow, then gouache straight out of the tube for closer snowflakes, to create depth. I then streaked the flat brush through some of the snowflakes in the same direction.

The sheep were rendered in a similar manner, although at the very end I scratched diagonally across them with a scalpel to give the impression of fast-driven snow.

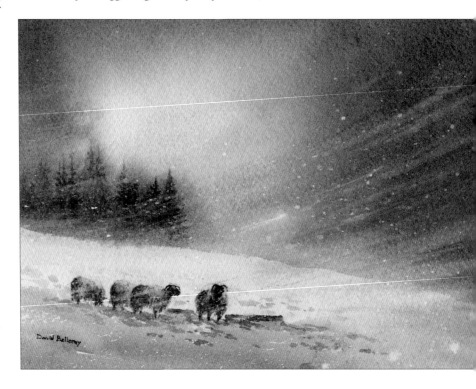

70

FARM IN SNOW

Intricate white details in a snow painting can be tricky to achieve, and this is where masking fluid really comes into its own, although it often needs tidying up a bit after removal, especially if it has been applied clumsily. In this demonstration, I show how the white features are created, including the usefulness of having a tube of white gouache handy.

Materials used

Saunders Waterford 640gsm (300lb) HP watercolour paper

Brushes: No. 10 sable round, large and small squirrel mops, no. 7 sable round, 13mm (½in) flat, no. 1 rigger, no. 4 and no. 3 sable round

Colours: Cobalt blue, cadmium red, Naples yellow, cadmium orange, alizarin crimson, burnt sienna, Indian red, burnt umber, yellow ochre, cadmium yellow pale, white gouache

Masking fluid and old brush

1 Draw the scene and mask the roofs and tops of walls with masking fluid. Add a few dabs of masking fluid to the trees to suggest snow. Use the no. 10 sable round to paint the snowy hillside in the background with cobalt blue and cadmium red. Allow to dry.

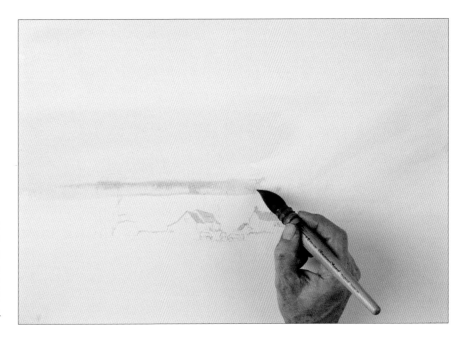

2 Use the large squirrel mop to sweep clean water across the background to just below the tree line and drop in Naples yellow on the left. Paint a line of cadmium orange beyond the trees to suggest a sliver of light.

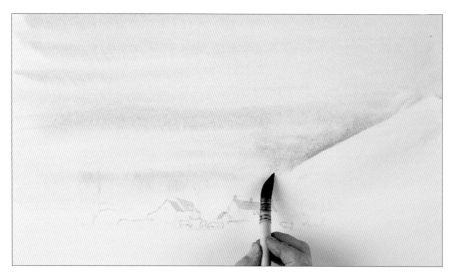

3 Paint cobalt blue and cadmium red wet into wet from the top of the sky downwards to blend with the yellow. Soften any hard edges that appear with a damp brush. Use a smaller squirrel mop with alizarin crimson and cobalt blue to define the mountain ridge, and blend it across the sky.

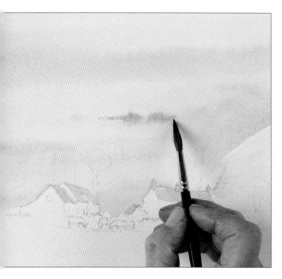

4 Wait until the sky is just damp and use the no. 7 sable round to dot in clouds with cadmium red and cobalt blue. Test at the edge of the picture to make sure the cloud wash does not spread too far in the damp background.

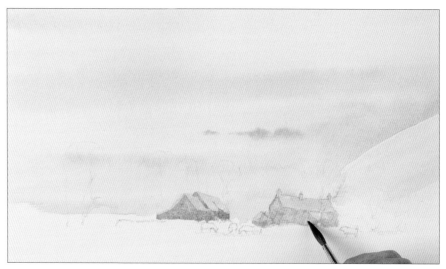

5 Paint the buildings with cobalt blue and burnt sienna, then drop in yellow ochre and alizarin crimson.

6 Use a damp 13mm (½in) flat brush to soften the line of the ridge.

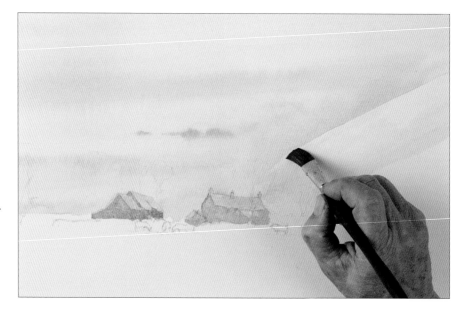

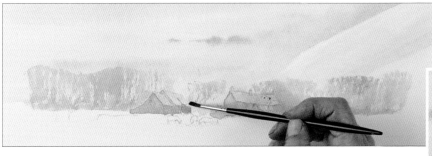
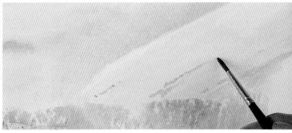

7 Mix burnt sienna and cobalt blue and use the no. 4 round to paint in the background trees. Use the same mix to suggest rocks showing through the snow in the ridge.

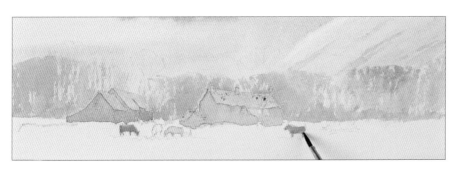
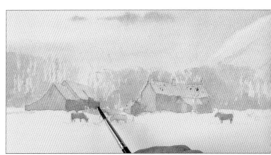

8 Paint some of the cows with Naples yellow with a touch of Indian red, then another two with burnt sienna.

9 Make a shadow mix of alizarin crimson and cobalt blue and paint the area between the buildings, then paint the shaded parts of the buildings with varying mixes of the same colours.

10 Use the no. 7 brush to paint this shadow mix along the treeline to the right of the buildings, and blend it upwards. Repeat to the left of the buildings.

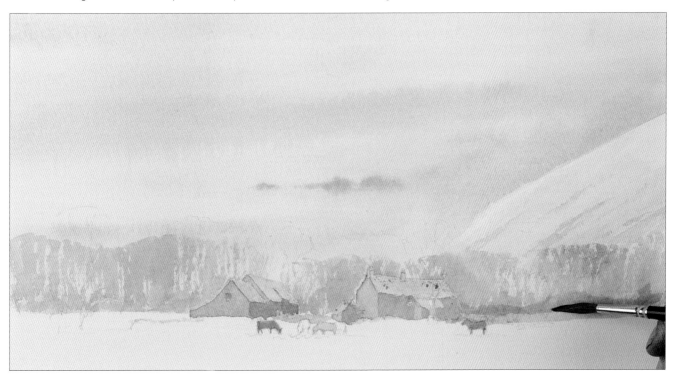

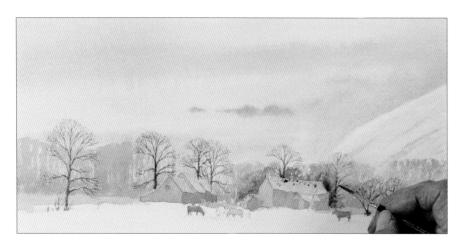

11 Use the no. 1 rigger and burnt umber with cobalt blue to paint trunks and branches on the background trees.

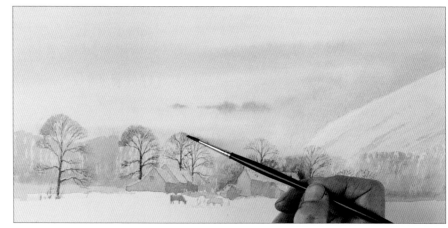

12 Mix cadmium red and cobalt blue and use the no. 4 round brush on its side to paint the twigwork of the trees.

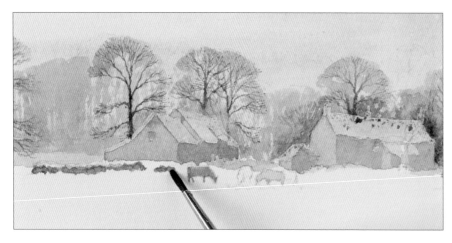

13 Paint the dry-stone wall with a mix of burnt sienna and cobalt blue, then drop in yellow ochre and alizarin crimson wet into wet.

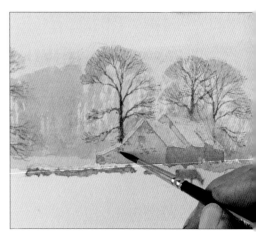

14 Suggest the darker stonework of the buildings with a mix of cobalt blue and burnt sienna, applied wet on dry.

15 Add the darkest details of the buildings such as doors, windows and shadows under the eaves with the same mix.

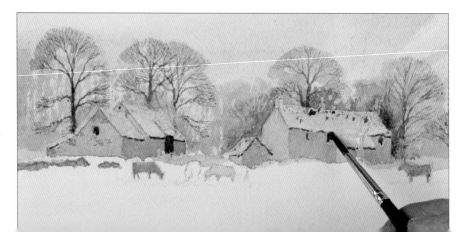

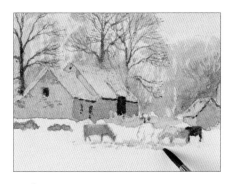

16 Add shade and detail to the cows with the same mix. Allow to dry. Paint yellow ochre under the cows for hay.

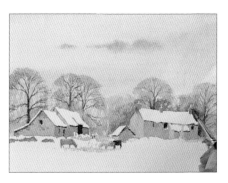

17 Remove the masking fluid. Use the no. 3 round brush to paint the chimneys with yellow ochre and the pots in Naples yellow.

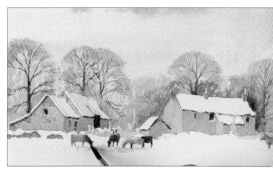

18 Paint the shadowed snowy roofs with alizarin crimson and cobalt blue. Paint the final cow with burnt umber and cobalt blue and add shadow on the others with the same mix.

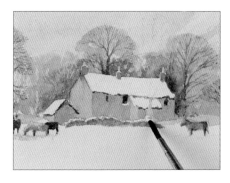

19 Paint the wall in front of the house with cobalt blue and burnt sienna, leaving white for the snow on top, then drop in yellow ochre and alizarin crimson wet into wet.

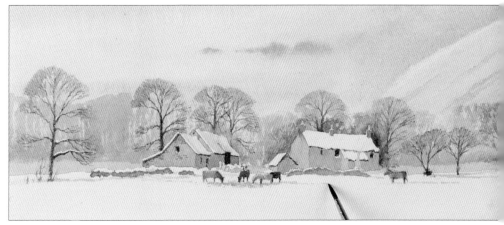

20 Use the shadow mix of alizarin crimson and cobalt blue to paint cast shadows from the trees, cows and chimneys.

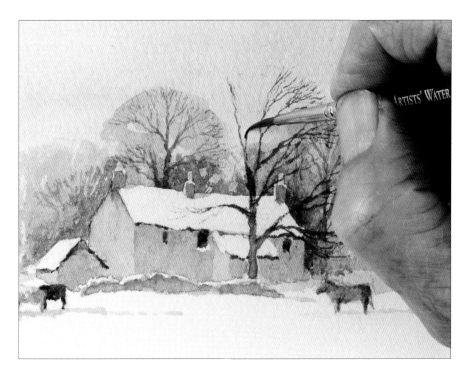

21 Mix cobalt blue and burnt sienna and paint the tree in front of the house with the no. 4 brush. While this is wet, change to the no. 3 sable round and drop in cadmium yellow pale. Continue painting twigs and branches with the brown mix.

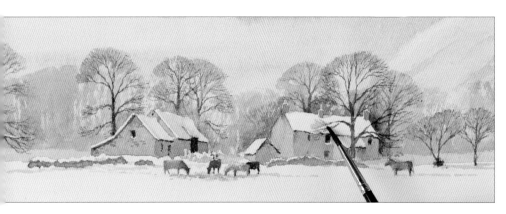

22 Paint the twigwork on the trees with cadmium red and cobalt blue, with the brush on its side and the dry-brush technique.

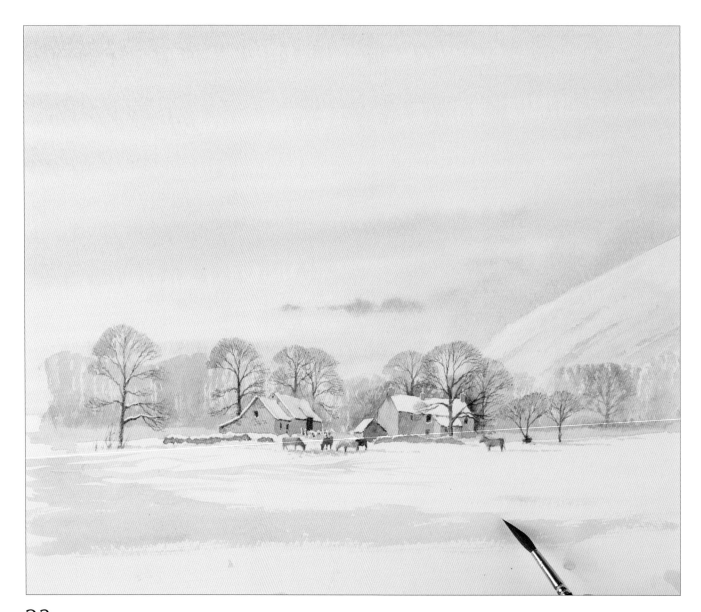

23 Strengthen the shadows beyond the house and on the buildings with a mix of alizarin crimson and cobalt blue. Use the no. 1 rigger to tidy up and add any final details. Change to the no. 7 round brush and paint cast shadows across the foreground snow from some imagined trees to the left of the scene, suggesting the contours of the land.

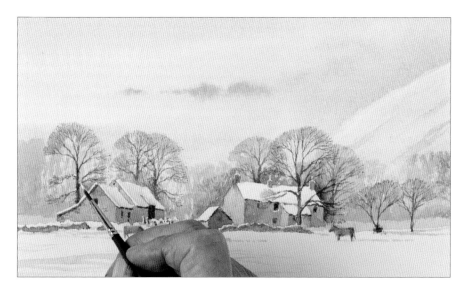

24 Step back from the painting to see what remains to be done. At this point, I darkened behind the snowy roofs with burnt sienna and cobalt blue, then added a little white gouache to suggest snow caught in the trees.

The finished painting.

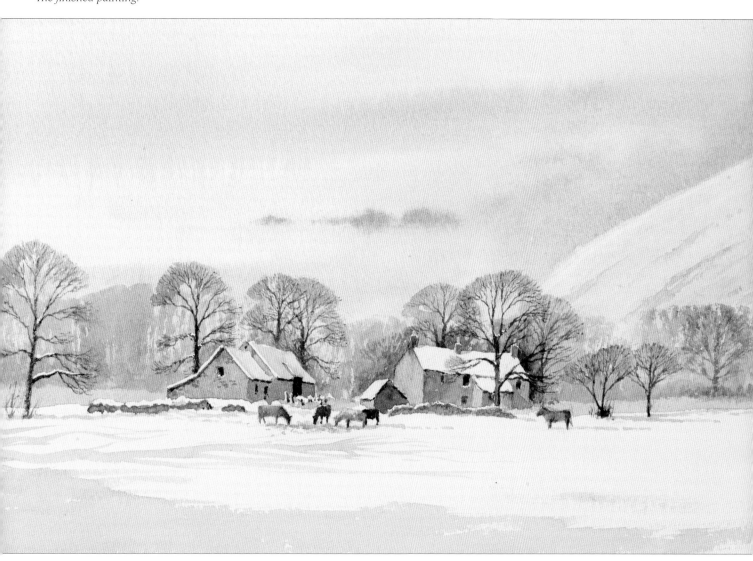

Spring

Getting outside and recording the lovely fresh colours of the springtime landscape is a rewarding and joyful exercise. You can still see the graceful lines of trees as buds emerge, the winter chill recedes and longer hours of daylight allow more time for sketching on location. Those overwhelming greens of the summer are still some way off. Choice of colours is an important consideration, as you do need to suggest spring freshness.

Seek out hints of spring and the coming of warmer weather. Note the brighter colours of grass and vegetation and the arrival of spring flowers, often set against the warm colours of dead leaves and branches. These make for interesting foregrounds. Nothing implies the onset of spring more evocatively than the sight of lambs in the fields. Tree blossom is another strong indicator of the arrival of spring, and can help to support a centre of interest.

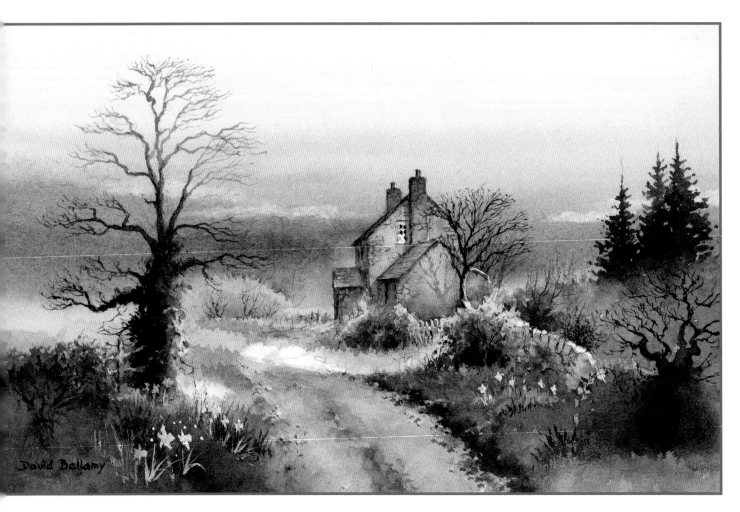

David Bellamy

Opposite

March Sunlight
17.8 x 24cm (7 x 9½in), 300gsm (140lb) Hot Pressed paper

In this scene, the shadows lengthen as the day draws to a close. I wanted to capture the feeling of early spring sunlight casting shadows across the building and lane, without making them too strong. I chose a Hot Pressed surface because it is excellent for sharp detail, and here I wanted the daffodils to stand out. They were rendered by applying masking fluid first, removing it once the dark green verges were dry, and then painting in some cadmium yellow pale, which stands out well against the dark green. As daffodils have hard-edged, angular petals, masking fluid is good this purpose.

Edge of the Wood
20.3 x 29.2cm (8 x 11½in), 300gsm (140lb) Not paper

Although there are still dead winter leaves around in this watercolour, signs of early spring in the form of lambs and primroses are evident. These are excellent features with which to soften the bleakness of a winter landscape, and as spring progresses, you can include blossom, bright yellow-greens and more flowers. Spring-time can be highly rewarding for those landscape painters who experience difficulties with the massed greens of summer.

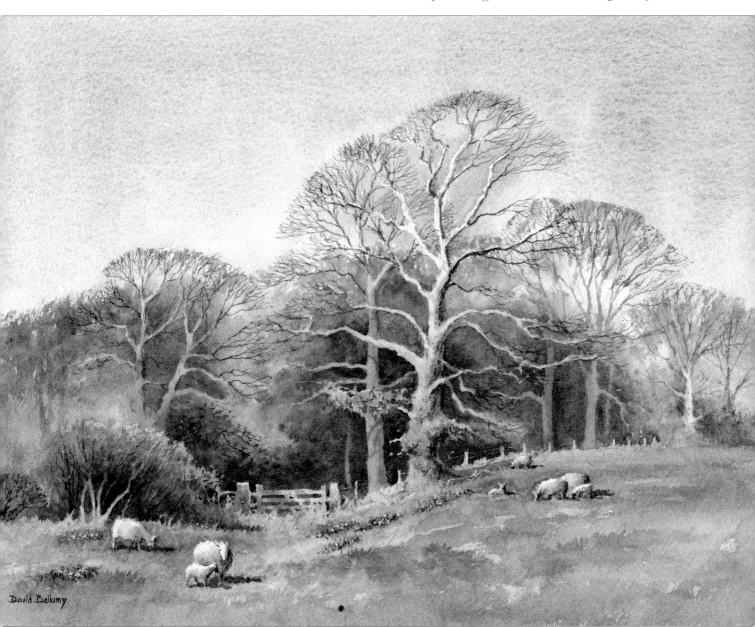

Spring colours

Keep your greens and yellows fresh and clean, as in the sketch of a stream at the bottom of this page. The chart below gives an idea of some good colour mixtures for this, but it is far from exhaustive. As you will see, I have also included a few mixtures of richer and perhaps duller colours, as these can be useful in places to offset the overall brightness. Pink blossom can easily be painted with a weak wash of alizarin crimson or quinacridone red. Colour in the landscape is, of course, considerably affected by light and shade, and cast shadow across bright foliage or a sea of bluebells can dramatically change the way the colour is perceived.

Mixing spring colours

The chart below shows colour combinations for spring greens, with a couple of warmer summer versions often prominent in late spring. By including green apatite genuine or lunar blue, you can create granulations which suggest foliage without any help from the artist!

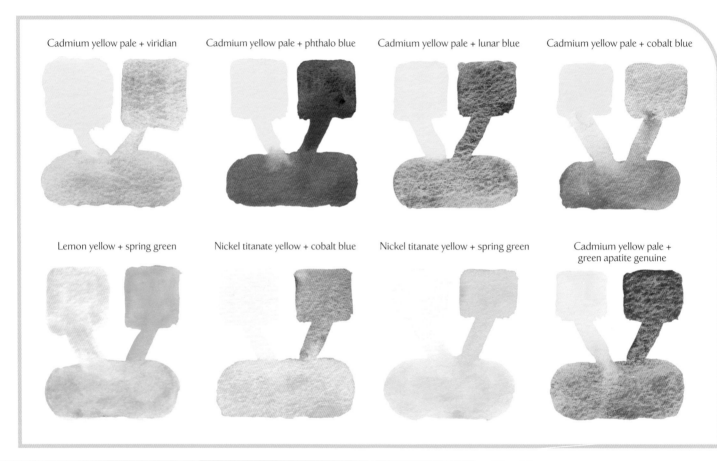

Cadmium yellow pale + viridian

Cadmium yellow pale + phthalo blue

Cadmium yellow pale + lunar blue

Cadmium yellow pale + cobalt blue

Lemon yellow + spring green

Nickel titanate yellow + cobalt blue

Nickel titanate yellow + spring green

Cadmium yellow pale + green apatite genuine

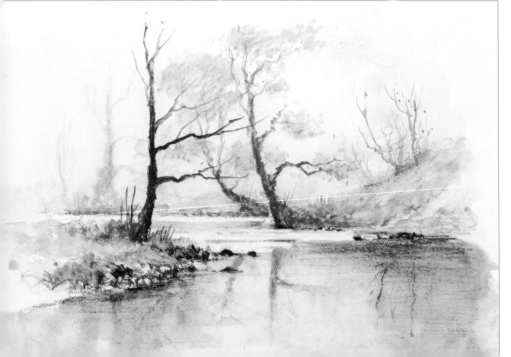

Placid stream

For this sketch, I used Derwent Inktense pencils, drawing first and then washing over with water. The fresh, bright greens give a strong impression of spring, with some trees still bare of leaves. You can combine these pencils with ordinary watercolours if you wish.

Injecting a feeling of spring

Young lambs, daffodils and primroses all suggest springtime, but here we look at two other strong indicators of this lovely time of year. Vast fields of bluebells have considerable impact, and are often seen at their best when sunlight is pouring through the trees to create patterns of light and shade across the blue masses, a subject we tackle below. Blossom is another harbinger of spring. Hawthorn blossom can totally transform the lower slopes of mountains, but here I use a couple of bushes to create a centre of interest in a Suffolk field.

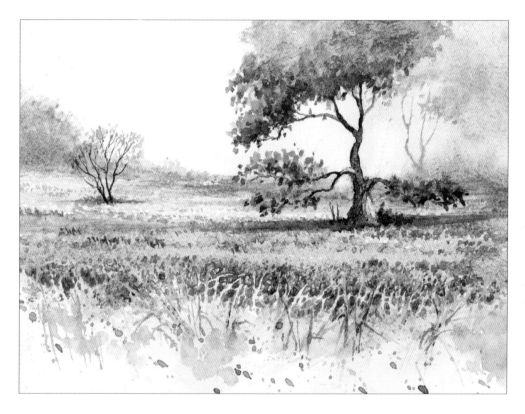

Bluebell Field
14 x 18cm (5½ x 7in) 300gsm (140lb) Not paper

While it is easy to make out the individual shapes of bluebells close to you, avoid detailing them as individual flowers. Try to create an overall impression of the mass with just a hint of detail in the closer ones. When these flowers are seen en masse, many tonal variations become apparent through dips in the ground or cast shadows, so use this to inject variety into a sea of bluebells.

The bluebells were painted with combinations of cobalt violet deep, ultramarine violet and French ultramarine,

Suffolk Blossom
25.4 x 35.5cm (10 x 14in) 425gsm (200lb) Rough paper

Blossom not only suggests springtime, but also helps to support a focal point. I have painted the scene much as it appeared on the day, though to create some life, I added a couple of pheasants. As the ploughed field was rather dull in colour, I used burnt sienna to warm it up a little.

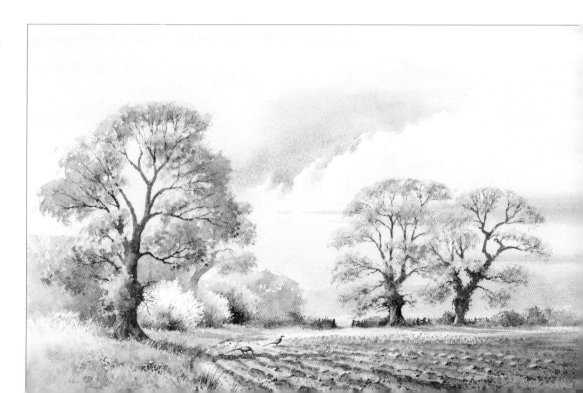

AFTER THE SPRING SHOWER

There is nothing quite like a spring shower to freshen up the landscape. I take every opportunity to record these effects, as they can give a painting such a lovely sense of mood. One of the main objectives in this demonstration is to show you how to suggest the wet surface of a country lane, and a touch of sparkle on something as mundane as a muddy field.

Materials used

Saunders Waterford 640gsm (300lb) Not watercolour paper

Brushes: Small and large squirrel mops, no. 10 sable round, no. 7 sable round, no. 3 rigger, no. 4 sable round, 6mm (¼in) flat, no. 1 rigger, no. 3 sable round

Colours: Cerulean blue, Naples yellow, alizarin crimson, cobalt blue, cadmium red, yellow ochre, cadmium yellow pale, burnt sienna, Indian red, light red, raw umber, new gamboge, cadmium orange, burnt umber, white gouache

Sponge

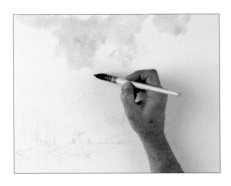

1 Use the small squirrel mop and cerulean blue to paint the sky, leaving lots of white for clouds. Do not apply water first, as you want some hard edges to appear. Soften the left-hand edges with a damp brush as these are away from the sun.

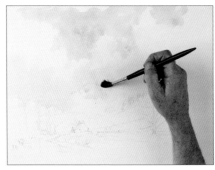

2 Change to the no. 10 sable round and paint a wet wash of Naples yellow in the lower sky and down over the distance. Drop in a little alizarin crimson to warm the colour and allow to dry.

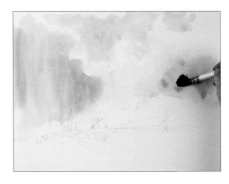

3 Wet the paper in the lower sky and distance using the large squirrel mop, then sweep down a mix of cobalt blue and cadmium red. Soften in places with a damp brush.

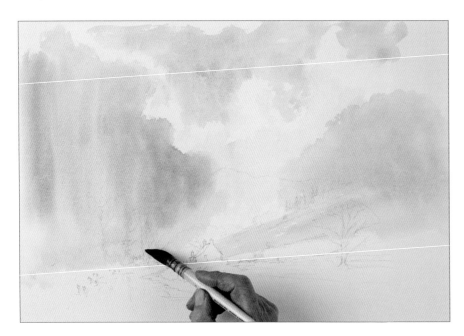

4 Paint yellow ochre from the right-hand cloud down to the building, then on the left over the foliage area. Add cadmium yellow pale in the middle distance.

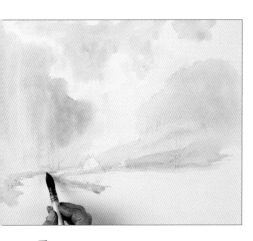

5 Mix cobalt blue with cadmium yellow pale and paint this on the fields near the house. Add Naples yellow below this, then paint the original mix in the area of the daffodils and along the road's edge. Allow to dry.

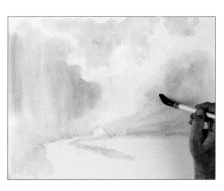

6 Use a damp sponge to soften the edge of the right-hand cloud, then paint on more cadmium red and cobalt blue with the large squirrel mop.

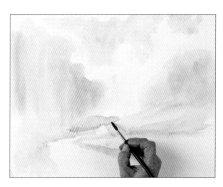

7 Paint the background trees with alizarin crimson and yellow ochre on the no. 7 brush, then add burnt sienna lower down.

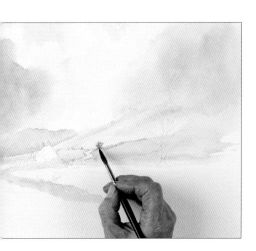

8 Paint a pale mix of cobalt blue and Indian red down the slope towards the house, indicating rough pasture. Drop in light red wet into wet.

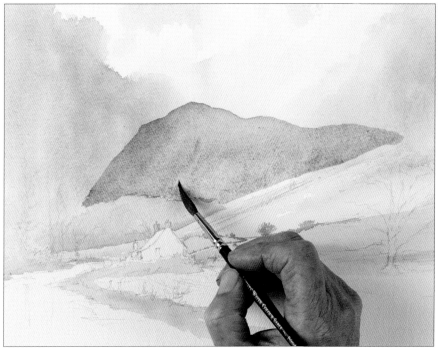

9 Change to the squirrel mop and paint the distant mountain with cobalt blue and burnt sienna with a little yellow ochre. Drop in yellow ochre wet into wet with the no. 7 brush.

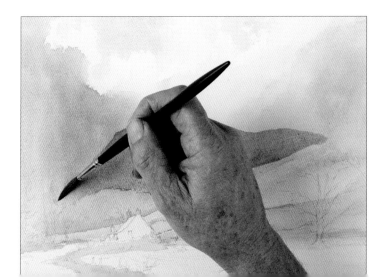

10 Soften the lower edge of the mountain with clean water as it goes behind the trees.

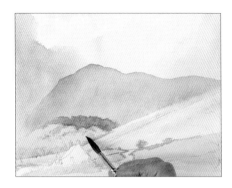

11 Mix yellow ochre and cobalt blue and use the no. 7 brush to paint the darker area of trees, then lift out some of the colour to texture the massed trees in front. Allow to dry.

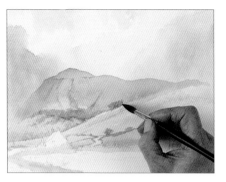

12 Use a sponge to subdue the darker trees, then use the yellow ochre and cobalt blue mix to suggest gullies on the distant mountain. Extend the distant line of trees with the same mix.

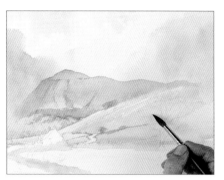

13 Stand back to assess the painting from time to time. At this point I decided that the right-hand slope needed to look more spring-like, so I brightened it with cadmium yellow pale and a little cobalt blue.

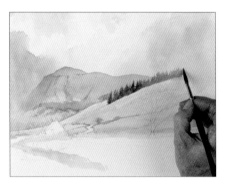

14 Paint the conifers on the right with raw umber and cobalt blue, varying the strength.

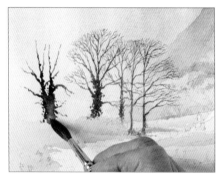

15 Use the tip of the no. 7 brush to paint the trees on the left with raw umber and cobalt blue for the trunks and the branches on the right, and burnt umber on the left. Suggest the ivy on some trunks and drop in new gamboge, then cadmium orange wet into wet.

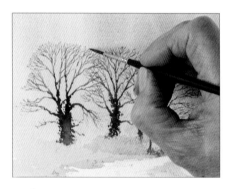

16 Use a no. 3 rigger and raw umber with cobalt blue to build up the finer branches.

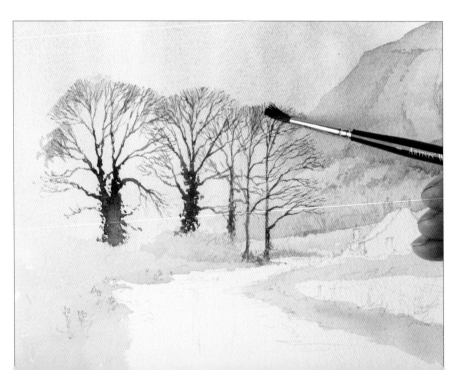

17 Mix burnt umber and cobalt blue and paint the twigwork of the trees with the no. 4 round brush on its side.

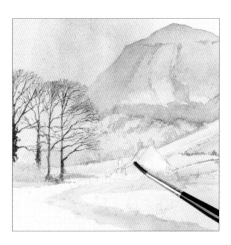

18 Paint the roof of the building with a very pale mix of cadmium red and cobalt blue.

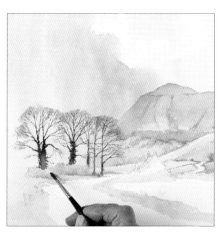

19 Paint yellow ochre and cobalt blue under the trees for the shaded part of the hedge. Add cadmium yellow pale for the lighter part.

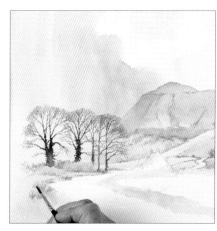

20 Add spots of light red for dead leaves under the trees, then mix cobalt blue with a little new gamboge to create the daffodil leaves coming forwards.

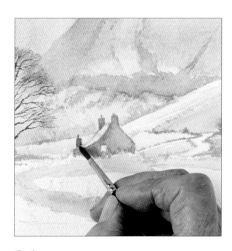

21 Paint the shaded side of the house with burnt umber and cobalt blue, then drop in Naples yellow wet into wet. Paint the chimneys in the same way.

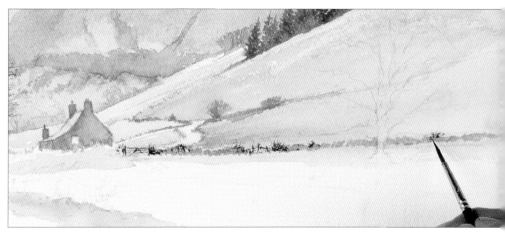

22 Paint the hedge with cobalt blue and new gamboge, then use the no. 3 round brush with cobalt blue and burnt umber to paint the gate, fenceposts and details in the hedge.

23 Continue painting the posts on the left of the house, the window panes and the tree behind the house.

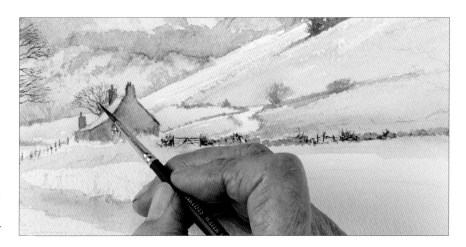

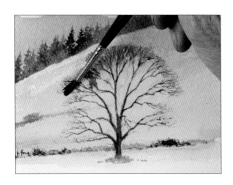
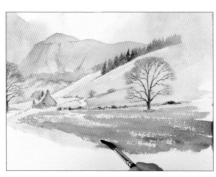
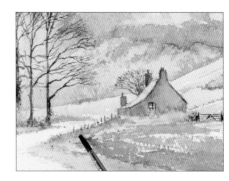

24 Use the no. 4 brush to paint the tree on the right with raw umber and cobalt blue, then drop in alizarin crimson. Change to the no. 1 rigger and a mix of burnt umber and cobalt blue to extend the branches and twigs. Use the no. 4 brush on its side to paint the twigwork with the same mix.

25 Use the no. 10 brush and burnt sienna to sweep in the ploughed field with the dry-brush technique, leaving speckles of white.

26 Paint the greenery in front of the house and along the fence with the no. 4 brush and cadmium yellow pale, then drop in raw umber.

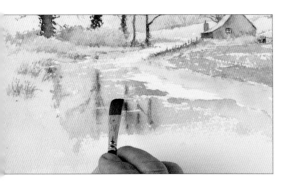

27 Use the no. 10 brush on its side to sweep cobalt blue and burnt umber from side to side across the foreground track, picking up the paper texture. While the paint is wet, paint reflections with a darker mix, then lift out colour with a just-damp 6mm (¼in) flat brush, suggesting ripples.

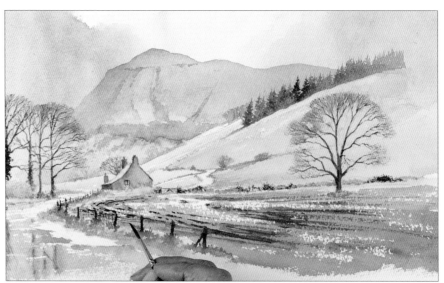

28 Brighten the grass verge beside the track with cadmium yellow pale and cobalt blue on the no. 4 brush, then use the no. 7 brush and burnt umber with a touch of cobalt blue to paint furrows and texture in the ploughed field. Add fenceposts with a darker mix of the same colours, then paint a darker mix of the previous green for grasses. Add netting to the fence with the no. 1 rigger and the brown mix.

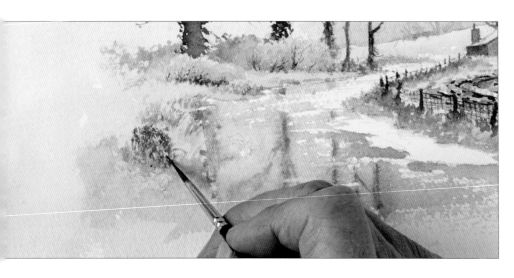

29 Paint the daffodils with white gouache, then cadmium yellow pale. Paint negatively around them with cobalt blue and cadmium yellow pale.

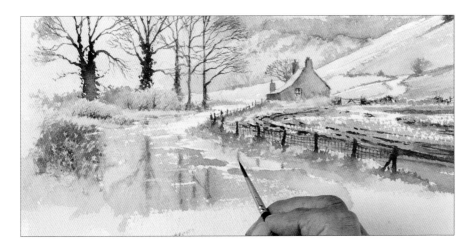

30 Clean up any pencil marks, then use the no. 7 brush and cobalt blue with cadmium red to add dark touches to the puddle, reflecting the sky. Add fencepost reflections to the road with burnt umber and cobalt blue.

The finished painting.

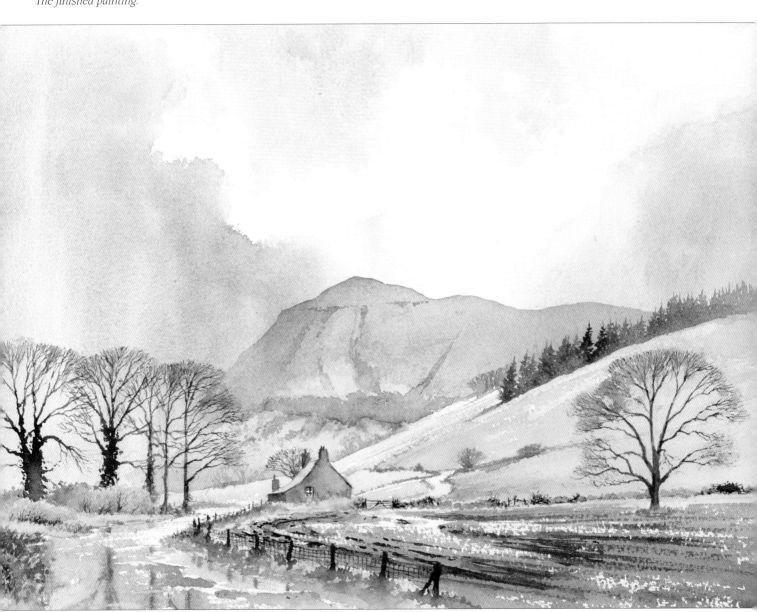

Planning paintings

Having read this book, you will no doubt be keen to get stuck into your own compositions. Working out your plan of action is best done with studio sketches based on sketches, photographs and memory, as discussed below.

Using sketches and photographs

Altering the subject

It is rare to come across the perfect scene as it should be painted, and here I show how I approach the process of making slight alterations to enhance the finished painting.

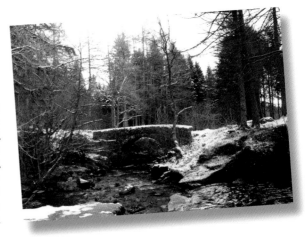

While this made a superb subject to paint, like so many woodland scenes, the photograph suffered from a dark and dismal mood, being enclosed by tall trees. My aim was to create more space and depth, change the lighting, convey a much warmer impression and improve the atmosphere. While I intended to retain the basic composition, I carried out a studio sketch (below) to clear a number of points in my mind. My changes mainly involved a different choice of colours and tonal values, plus a few minor adjustments to features, rather than major compositional alterations.

Studio sketch

I often add notes as reminders to myself, but here I have included them mainly to show my conclusions on how I would proceed. Exchanging the left-hand trees for a smaller bush, lowering the ground to the left of the bridge so that it does not coincide with the parapet, and reducing the height of the right-hand trees helped to avoid awkward relationships, but more importantly, I felt the bridge needed to stand out more by lightening the far bank viewed through the arch of the structure.

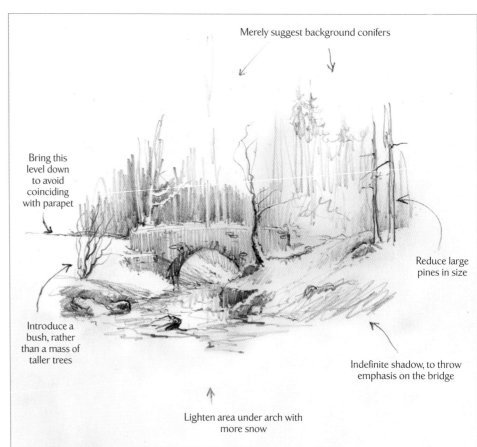

Merely suggest background conifers

Bring this level down to avoid coinciding with parapet

Introduce a bush, rather than a mass of taller trees

Reduce large pines in size

Indefinite shadow, to throw emphasis on the bridge

Lighten area under arch with more snow

Woodland Bridge
17.8 x 25.4cm (7 x 10in), 300gsm (140lb) Not paper

My first decision was to change the direction of the light source from right to left, so that the front of the bridge would be lighter, and weak cast shadows could be placed for the bridge's left-hand supporting buttress and the tree in front of the structure. Before applying paint, I covered the parapet of the bridge, some of the tops of the boulders, and the main tree branches with masking fluid to retain the intricate whites. I suggested a misty background by inserting the conifers on either side of the central mass with a wet-into-wet application of cobalt blue and cadmium red. This achieved a greater sense of space and depth. I took this wash right across to the right-hand side of the composition, weakening it as I went, and then cooled it with weak Winsor blue. This threw more warmth into the centre of the work.

When the paper had dried, I painted in the central background mass of trees in a stronger tone, thus pushing the conifers I had already painted into the distance. For the bridge itself, I used the cobalt blue plus cadmium red mixture, but dropped a little yellow ochre and some light red into the wash before it dried. Built of old red sandstone, the bridge does reveal a lot of red, especially in sunlight. When it had dried, I suggested a few of the stones with a fine rigger, putting more emphasis on the stones around the arch of the bridge.

I reduced the tree and rock detail and simplified the ground area, especially in the left-hand foreground. A very weak wash of Winsor blue was washed across the river and allowed to dry thoroughly before a second, much deeper wash of the same colour was applied, leaving some of the first wash to show through as streaks across the water. While this second wash remained wet, an even darker application was placed under the bridge to hint at a dark reflection. In a running current, reflections generally do not need to be highly accurate. I painted in the foreground ripples with the same dark colour, using a no. 6 round brush. Finally I removed the masking fluid and spotted in a few flecks of white gouache to indicate snow on the branches.

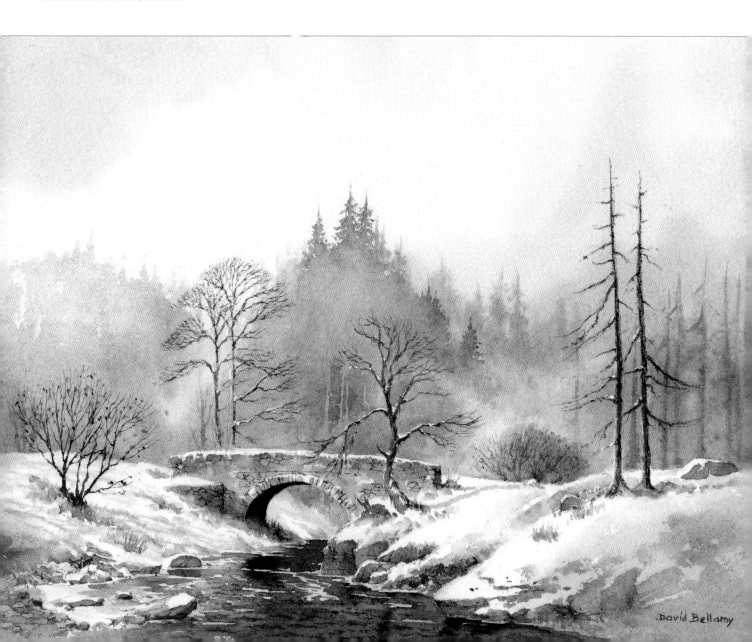

David Bellamy

The importance of the studio sketch

In many cases it is easy enough to work directly from a sketch or photograph without any problems, but what if you want to beef up the composition with stronger tones, inject a different atmosphere, add figures or animals, or make changes to various features? This is where the studio sketch is invaluable, and with complicated subjects it is worth doing several before choosing your course of action. Studio sketches can be a simple pencil sketch – use a soft grade such as 3B or 4B, charcoal or water-soluble graphite pencils. I sometimes use Derwent Inktense blocks, water-soluble ink blocks which can give a quick, broad image over which you can wash water.

Having a collection of sketches and photographs of objects, animals, figures and various features to add to your composition will greatly enhance your paintings. These can be used to replace less attractive features, so long as they are in keeping with the subject matter, and it pays to constantly build up your reservoir of images. Used in combination with the studio sketch, they will enhance your compositions.

I made alterations to the above scene to improve the composition. I often do this automatically, as in this case, but if you are inexperienced, or presented with a more complicated subject, then a studio sketch is essential, as the following example will show.

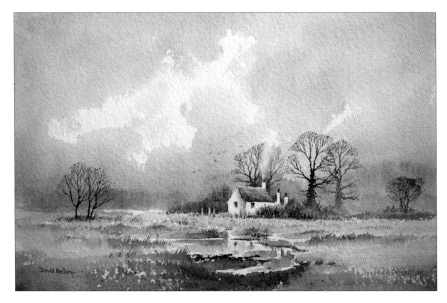

Cottage near the River Wey, Surrey
20.3 x 28cm (8 x 11in)

I felt that this painting needed a little tweaking to strengthen the composition: the left-hand distant trees were deliberately faded away, even though they could be clearly seen; I added rising smoke from the chimney to suggest human presence; the gable end of the cottage was rendered with a graduated wash to make it stand out; I varied the tones on the right-hand trees to avoid monotony, and finally added a puddle for foreground interest.

Aberedw in Autumn

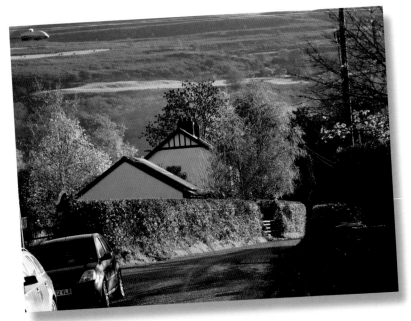

The reference photograph

This scene, near my home in Wales, has many attractive features, but would benefit from a number of changes to turn it into a more exciting composition.

90

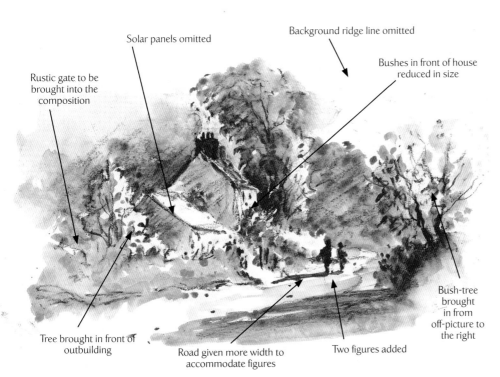

Rustic gate to be brought into the composition

Solar panels omitted

Background ridge line omitted

Bushes in front of house reduced in size

Tree brought in front of outbuilding

Road given more width to accommodate figures

Two figures added

Bush-tree brought in from off-picture to the right

The studio sketch

Based on the photograph and original sketch, this is a rough studio sketch done with a water-soluble ink block, then washed over with water. This helped me to work out the tones and lighting, which is coming from the right. At the end I put in a couple of figures to see if they improved the composition, and moved in a bush-tree which was actually too far over to the right to be seen in the photograph. I decided to bring the left-hand tree slightly forward, in front of the outbuilding, to break up the hard lines. I also reduced the size of those in front of the house to give the building more prominence.

Aberedw in Autumn: the finished painting
15.3 x 23cm (6 x 9in)

The neatly cut hedgerow jarred with my sense of wild chaos, so I introduced a more uneven version, left out the solar panels on the outbuilding and created more space on either side. Background ridges can sometimes look awkward in a painting, so I brought in some mist to eliminate that problem. After further deliberation, I included two figures chatting in front of the house. I also darkened the small tree on the right to suggest a greater sense of depth in the composition, as dark tones tend to push the rest of the painting into the distance.

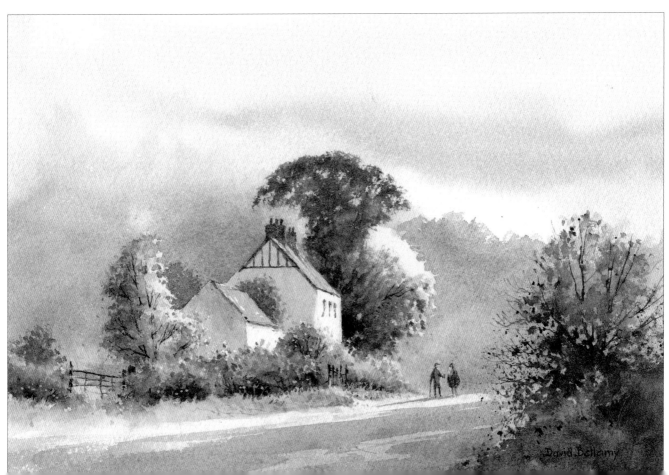

David Bellamy

Further techniques

Using spatter

The spatter technique can be extremely effective for adding interest and, because it is less controlled, a sense of spontaneity. It can be used for a confined area such as the extremities of a bush or vegetation, or for a larger spread across a foreground, to suggest roughness. As the spattered blobs can fly off in all directions, you need to mask off areas where you don't want them. An old toothbrush is excellent for creating spatter, but here I show other methods.

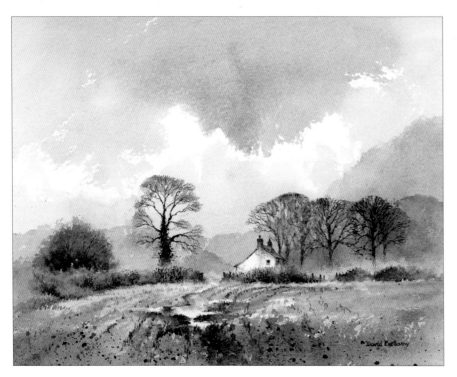

Pembrokeshire Farm
20.3 x 28cm (8 x 11in), 300gsm (140lb)
Not paper

In this painting of a farm in Wales, I used a no. 8 round sable brush, charged with a fluid mix of French ultramarine and burnt umber, and I brought the brush down sharply onto the handle of another brush to induce a jolt which spattered the wet paint across the foreground. Sometimes I use more than one colour to spatter an area.

Edge Top Farm, Longnor – watercolour sketch on cartridge paper

I don't normally spatter over snow, but in this watercolour sketch done on the spot in the English Peak District, I felt it would liven things up a little. The character of spatter is greatly affected by the type of brush you employ, the angle of approach, and whether you strike the brush against another object, as in the painting above, or use your finger or a knife to drag through the bristles of the brush. Here I simply loaded a no. 6 round sable with fluid paint, and holding it a couple of inches above the paper, flicked the brush with my first finger, adjusting the angle of the brush and flick of the finger to create a slightly more horizontal trajectory for the left-hand spattering.

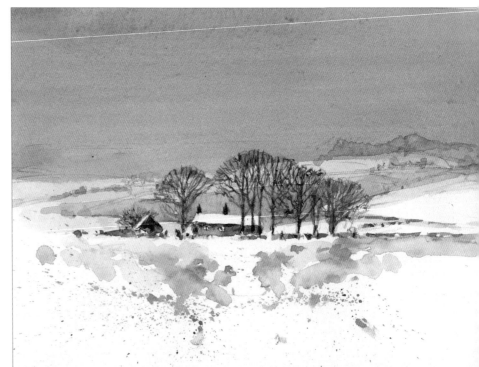

Including figures

The addition of figures into a landscape can boost its impact immeasurably, and is almost vital in town or village scenes. A splash of red is always welcome where colours are muted, but beware of clothing farmers in bright colours, as it somehow does not fit their image.

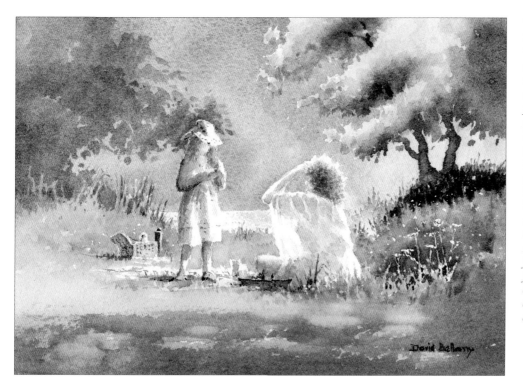

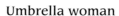

The Picnic

15.2 x 20.3cm (6 x 8in), 640gsm (200lb) Not paper

People caught in strong sunlight make interesting subjects. These two were from different parts of a large group of people enjoying late summer sunshine at a wedding. Observing how the light falls onto clothing, hair and limbs is critical. Try not to make it too busy. If you looked harder, you would see much more detail in the child's dress and hat, but rendering it all would detract from the sense of strong light falling on it. Note the halo effect on the adult's hair, an essential feature where you encounter backlighting.

Umbrella woman

This figure's stance reveals that she is fighting the wind and it is not a pleasant day. An appropriate stance can really add authenticity to your work.

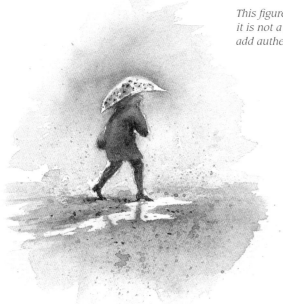

Walking couple

Here the couple are hunched up, huddling together against the elements. Naturally, they are well wrapped-up.

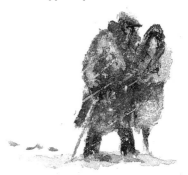

Adjusting the colour temperature

There are times when you reach the end of a painting and you can clearly see that the overall effect is too cold and uninviting. All is not lost, as you can introduce a warm transparent glaze over the whole or part of the work. Make sure the painting is completely dry – leave it overnight if you wish – and then decide where you will apply the glaze. You may decide to cover the whole painting. Permanent rose, quinacridone red and permanent alizarin crimson are excellent transparent colours which will warm up a painting. Mix up a generous pool of colour – quite a bit more than you estimate you will require, as there is nothing worse than having to stop and mix more paint in the middle of a large wash. Test the glaze over part of a watercolour that you will not need any more, and when you are satisfied, lay it over the painting with a large soft-haired mop brush. As with normal washes, you may wish to graduate the glaze by adding more water to the mixture in places.

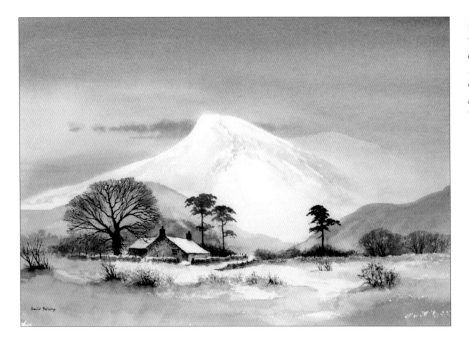

Mountain Farm – first version

This painting was originally done as a demonstration, and when I looked at it some time later, it struck me that it appeared rather cold, and the central part was glaringly white between the Caledonian pines.

Mountain Farm – second version

30.5 x 38cm (12 x 15in), 640gsm (300lb) Not paper

With a very fluid wash of French ultramarine and alizarin crimson, I glazed the sky and lower mountain passages to suggest an evening scene, with the alizarin crimson warming up the composition considerably. I also strengthened the lower hills and accentuated the smoke rising from the farmhouse. The foreground snow bank also needed darkening to be in keeping with the time of day. This method not only warms the scene but can also suggest reflected colours on a passage of snow.

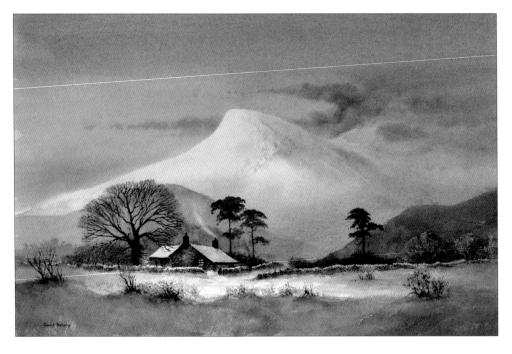

Vignettes

The vignette method can be extremely effective in simplifying a composition or providing a fresh and more spontaneous result. The earliest vignettes were generally those with the edges around the painting softened, which you can carry out with gradated brushwork, or by sponging gently round the edges. However, perhaps the most exciting and fresh results are achieved by deliberately planning how much of the scene you will leave unpainted, and where you will place any isolated shapes as in the foreground poppies here. If you are reticent about leaving areas of white paper unpainted, try working on a sheet of tinted paper.

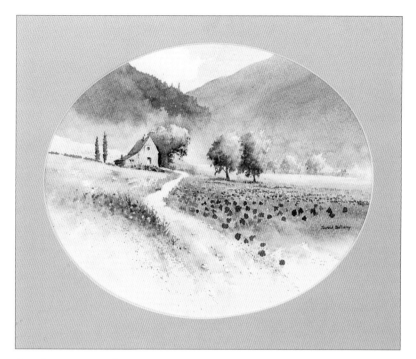

Dordogne Poppies
21.5 x 25.4cm (8½ x 10in) 300gsm (140lb) Not paper

Using an elliptical mount round a vignetted painting diminishes the amount of blank space in the foreground. In this scene I have faded out the closer grasses and just included a few poppies in the immediate foreground, adding a little spatter here and there. Spattering works well with the vignette technique.

Farm in the Clwydian Hills
20.3 x 30.5cm (8 x 12in) 300gsm (140lb) Not paper

Where there is a lot of repetitive detail in the foreground, the vignette technique is an excellent alternative to rendering everything you see before you. Simply fade out the detail as indicated in this composition. You can paint on white paper, or, if preferred, lay a weak wash of a light colour such as raw sienna or yellow ochre, and let it dry before painting in the detail, fading it out as it approaches the viewer.

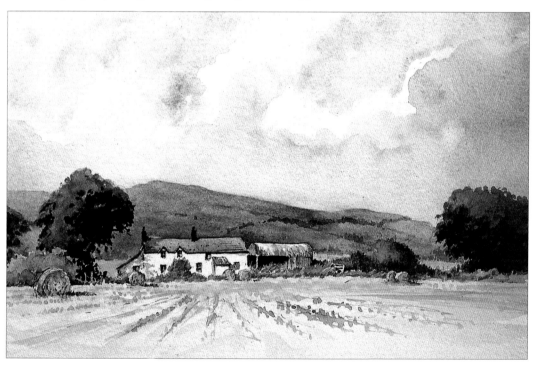

Index

animal 67, 90
atmosphere 7, 66, 68, 88, 90
autumn 7, 36–47, 90, 91

brushes 10, 12, 13, 20, 30, 42, 56, 71, 82
building 16, 27, 28, 29, 30, 31, 37, 40, 51, 52, 53, 68, 72, 74, 76, 79, 82, 85, 91
bush(es) 12, 33, 38, 39, 42, 54, 60, 67, 81, 88, 91, 92

centre of interest 19, 38, 49, 64, 78, 81
cloud 29, 41, 56, 72, 82, 83
colours
  autumn 7, 36, 39, 40, 41
  cool 16, 56, 65, 68, 89
  opaque 8
  rogue 30, 52
  spring 16, 78, 80, 84
  summer 16, 28, 37, 78, 79, 80
  transparent 8, 19, 20, 21, 30, 31, 39, 41, 94
  warm 7, 16, 17, 27, 28, 37, 39, 40, 41, 44, 48, 52, 53, 56, 58, 62, 65, 66, 70, 78, 80, 82, 89, 94
  winter 45, 52, 56
composition 14, 16, 18, 19, 30, 36, 38, 40, 41, 51, 52, 56, 63, 64, 65, 68, 70, 89, 90, 91, 94, 95

dry-stone wall 13, 29, 60, 65, 74

farm 29, 37, 51, 53, 63, 64, 71–77, 92, 93, 94, 95
field 16, 29, 30, 48, 52, 53, 63, 78, 81, 82, 83, 86
figure 65, 90, 91, 93
focal point 27, 28, 29, 30, 40, 52, 53, 81
foliage 6, 17, 18, 19, 20, 21, 22, 23, 24, 25, 26, 27, 36, 37, 39, 42, 44, 45, 46, 48, 80, 83

grasses 29, 34, 35, 43, 51, 61, 86, 95

highlight 8, 14, 19, 26, 29, 34, 48, 56, 58, 64, 67
hill 17, 29, 36, 48, 51, 62, 63, 64, 71, 78, 95

Impressionists 6

lake 13, 20, 41, 56, 58, 59, 60
Lake District 41, 56

lighting 7, 27, 28, 53, 66, 88, 91, 93, 96
  backlighting 27, 93

masking fluid 11, 20, 21, 23, 27, 30, 31, 39, 42, 45, 46, 53, 55, 63, 66, 68, 71, 75, 79, 89
mist/misty 6, 7, 20, 27, 30, 42, 66, 68, 69, 89, 91
mood 6, 7, 14, 27, 28, 38, 64, 82, 88
moor(land) 19, 30–35, 51, 62, 63
mountain 6, 13, 14, 19, 36, 41, 50, 55, 56–61, 62, 72, 81, 83, 84, 94

negative shapes 49, 54

Peak District 92
photograph 7, 14, 19, 20, 29, 36, 40, 50, 54, 68, 88, 90, 91

reflection 6, 17, 22, 25, 46, 48, 65, 66, 86, 87, 89
ripples 26, 46, 86, 89
river 17, 27, 38, 66, 89, 90
rock 16, 17, 20, 21, 23, 24, 25, 33, 34, 38, 41, 43, 45, 46, 47, 50, 56, 58, 73, 89
roof 14, 30, 31, 32, 33, 49, 51, 71, 75, 77, 85

Scottish Highlands 7, 70
shadow 14, 16, 17, 18, 19, 23, 24, 27, 28, 29, 31, 33, 35, 40, 41, 46, 48, 53, 55, 59, 60, 63, 64, 66, 69, 73, 76, 79, 80, 81, 88, 89
sketch(ing) 6, 7, 8, 9, 11, 14, 17, 18, 19, 20, 28, 29, 30, 36, 40, 50, 51, 54, 62, 64, 65, 68, 78, 80, 88, 90, 91, 92
sky/skies 14, 27, 30, 41, 42, 48, 55, 56, 63, 64, 65, 66, 68, 70, 72, 82, 87, 94
snow 6, 7, 16, 41, 48, 51, 62, 63, 64, 65, 66, 67, 68, 70, 71–77, 89, 92, 94
sponge 11, 26, 38, 56, 69, 82, 83, 84
spring 7, 18, 78–87
stream 24, 25, 42, 80
summer 6, 7, 14–35, 56, 93
sunlight/sunshine 6, 7, 14, 16, 18, 28, 29, 30, 35, 37, 42, 48, 50, 53, 64, 68, 79, 81, 89, 93

techniques
  dry-brush 20, 22, 38, 44, 46, 48, 56, 62, 76, 86
  glaze 46, 55, 57, 61, 69, 94
  lift(ing) out 13, 46, 84, 86
  lost and found 66

negative painting 13, 14, 18, 23, 33, 34, 49, 54, 55, 59, 66, 86
scratch(ing) out 26, 29, 34, 35, 40, 66, 70
spattered/spatter(ing) 11, 19, 21, 34, 39, 47, 51, 60, 61, 70, 92, 95
wash(es) 8, 9, 10, 11, 13, 17, 20, 23, 29, 30, 38, 39, 40, 41, 42, 43, 44, 45, 48, 49, 50, 51, 54, 56, 60, 61, 63, 64, 66, 67, 68, 70, 72, 80, 82, 89, 90, 94, 95
wax resist 30, 33, 63
wet into wet 17, 18, 20, 21, 22, 23, 32, 34, 38, 41, 42, 44, 45, 46, 47, 56, 57, 59, 66, 72, 74, 75, 83, 84, 85, 89
wet on dry 18, 57, 74
texture 8, 9, 12, 13, 18, 19, 21, 22, 29, 30, 31, 32, 33, 34, 44, 45, 46, 47, 48, 60, 61, 84, 86
tone 40, 42, 44, 46, 47, 51, 60, 63, 64, 66, 69, 89, 90, 91
tree 6, 12, 13, 16, 17, 18, 19, 20, 27, 29, 31, 32, 33, 36, 37, 38, 40, 41, 42, 43, 44, 45, 46, 48, 50, 51, 52, 53, 54, 55, 56, 59, 60, 63, 65, 66, 68, 69, 70, 71, 73, 74, 75, 76, 77, 78, 80, 81, 83, 84, 85, 86, 88, 89, 90, 91
  branch(es) 18, 19, 24, 27, 36, 41, 45, 47, 48, 54, 55, 59, 63, 66, 68, 74, 75, 78, 84, 86, 87
  trunk 13, 18, 19, 27, 33, 36, 41, 43, 44, 46, 48, 52, 54, 59, 66, 68, 69, 74, 84

village 6, 28, 93

Wales 90, 92
waterfall 20–26, 38, 42–47
water-soluble ink block 11, 64, 91
white gouache 8, 14, 19, 30, 34, 35, 55, 70, 71, 77, 82, 86, 89
winter 6, 7, 36, 37, 40, 42, 44, 48–77, 78, 79
working outdoors 6, 50

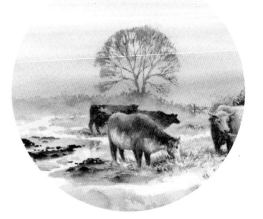